Linn's
Stamp Identifier

**Edited by
Donna O'Keefe**

Published by *Linn's Stamp News*, the largest and most informative stamp newspaper in the world. *Linn's* is owned by Amos Press Inc., 911 Vandemark Road, Sidney, Ohio 45365. Amos Press also publishes *Scott Stamp Monthly* and the Scott line of catalogs. Cover design by Veronica Schreiber.

Library of Congress Cataloging-in-Publication Data

Linn's stamp identifier / edited by Donna O'Keefe
    p. cm.
   ISBN 0-940403-52-8
   1. Postage-stamps--Identification--Handbooks, manuals, etc.
I. O'Keefe, Donna. II. Title: Stamp identifier.
HE6215.L566 1993
759.56--dc20   93-2693
                                                      CIP

Contents

Introduction

Linn's Stamp Identifier is the stamp identifier to end all stamp identifiers. Numerous stamp identifiers have been produced in the past by various publishers and organizations. All, however, seem to suffer from various weaknesses. In most, the listings of stamp inscriptions are inaccurate or out of date, or both. In others, the stamp illustrations are tiny and impossible to read, requiring a magnifying glass to see the inscriptions on the stamps. These faults defeat the purpose of an identifier, which is to help the collector determine the origin of his stamp with as little effort as possible. Until now, the stamp identifiers on the market have provided little help to the collector.

After examining the identifiers currently in print, the editors of *Linn's* realized that we were in the position to create the most definitive, easy-to-use, accurate identifier ever available. An identifier that works for the collector, rather than one that forces a collector to work to use it. We have capitalized on our numerous resources here at *Linn's* to produce what we feel is the best identifier on the market.

Linn's Stamp Identifier has been two years in the making. The listing of stamp inscriptions is as current as possible. We extend our heartfelt gratitude to C.C. Wright and the Greater Eugene (Oregon) Stamp Society for months of research in compiling the alphabetical listing of stamp inscriptions that appears in this book. This listing is keyed to the Scott *Standard Postage Stamp Catalogue* and is most useful in guiding the collector to the appropriate country in the catalog. The society has taken great pains to assure the accuracy of this listing of inscriptions.

Our special thanks also to Varro Tyler, an undisputed expert in the field of worldwide forgeries and author of the classic *Philatelic Forgers: Their Lives and Works*. Varro spent many hours checking the accuracy of *Linn's Stamp Identifier* listing and offering his valued advice.

The Fiscal Philatelic Foundation gave permission to reprint the alphabets of India from its scholarly work *The Court Fee and Revenue Stamps of the Princely States of India* by Adolph Koeppel and Raymond D. Manners, for which we are grateful.

Linn's staffers Bill Jones and Fred Baumann spent many hours identifying the stamps pictured in this book. The more than 500 illustrations are large and clear to enable the collector to find his stamp at a glance, without the need for a magnifying glass. The illustrations are grouped into categories with the collector in mind. We have constantly asked ourselves, "Where would the collector first look to find this stamp?" "What categories make it easiest for the average collector to identify his stamp?"

Linn's Stamp Identifier has been designed with the average collector in mind. Whether a child or an adult, any collector should be able to sit down with his mixture of stamps and, with this book, determine the origins of even the most obscure stamps. We are convinced that collectors will find this book to be one of the most useful reference tools ever available to collectors.

How to use this book

This book is designed to enable the collector to identify a given stamp by asking and answering fundamental questions about it.

Is it an adhesive postage stamp? What evidence is there that it is? And, if it is not a postage stamp, what could it be? If it is a postage stamp, what stamp-issuing entity (usually a country) created it?

By discovering the answers to these questions, step by step, *Linn's Stamp Identifier* should enable you to answer the final question — which stamp is it? — using the multivolume Scott *Standard Postage Stamp Catalogue* for worldwide stamps and the Scott *Specialized Catalogue of United States Stamps* for postal paper from the United States.

This slender text is no substitute for the thousands of pages of information gathered over more than a century and a quarter and presented in the Scott catalog and other catalogs. It is intended, instead, to help the user find his way around in these more massive references.

Given the limitations of space it is impossible to list, let alone depict, every kind of stamplike object that the worldwide collector can come across. We have nevertheless tried to indicate the characteristics of most broad classes of such items.

At the heart of this guide are the alphabetized listings that begin on page 1. To identify a stamp, first examine it carefully. Does it bear a name that appears to be the country or entity that issued the stamp? If so, check the appropriate Scott catalog for a listing of that country's stamps. Once you have located the country of origin of a postage stamp, a specific catalog listing may be sought by consulting the Index and Identifier section located in the back of the Scott multivolume catalog or, in the case of U.S. items, the table of contents section in the front of the Scott U.S. specialized catalog.

If the name of a country doesn't appear on the stamp, use *Linn's Stamp Identifier* to determine the origin of the stamp.

First, pay close attention to the inscriptions on the stamp. This book contains an alphabetical listing of more than 2,000 inscriptions that appear on stamps. It is highly likely that you will find your stamp's inscription in this listing.

In the alphabetical listing, the inscription is followed by the name of the stamp-issuing entity. If the name of the entity is in italics, this indicates that the entity is listed in one of the Scott catalogs. You should be able to identify the stamp by locating it in one of the catalogs. If the name doesn't appear in italics, the entity is not listed by Scott. To learn more about the stamp, you will need to consult a specialized reference.

If you can't find the inscription in the alphabetical listing or if the inscription is in characters of a non-Roman alphabet (i.e., Arabic, Cyrillic or Greek), consult the pages of illustrations beginning on page 60 of *Linn's Stamp Identifier*. Greek and Cyrillic alphabets are shown on page 56. The alphabets of India appear on pages 57-59. While we have not attempted any similar treatment of Arabian and Oriental languages, you'll find stamps representing these regions pictured on pages 62-67 and 68-78, respectively.

Linn's Stamp Identifier includes 65 pages of illustrations of some of the more troublesome designs. For the most part, the illustrations are organized by the inscriptions on the stamps. For example, stamps bearing inscriptions that appear to be Arabic are shown under the heading "Arabic inscriptions."

More than 500 stamps are pictured in the Difficult-to-identify stamps section, many featuring non-Roman characters. We have grouped together stamps with similar inscriptions, even though the issuing entities may be from different parts of the world. For example, stamps bearing inscriptions in a language used predominantly in Europe are illustrated under a category titled "European language inscriptions." A stamp may be pictured in the "European language inscriptions" category even though the issuing entity may not be located in Europe. A collector who has a stamp with an inscription in French is more likely to begin looking for the stamp among French stamps or among stamps with similar inscriptions.

Check the table of contents on page iv for the category most likely to describe your stamp.

If the stamp doesn't fall into a particular language-inscription category, it is pictured according to its use. These categories include bogus stamps, locals, seals and labels, stamps bearing no country name and telegraph stamps. Sections also are included for Africa, North America, and South and Central America.

Linn's Stamp Identifier contains listings for some stamp-issuing entities too recent in origin to have been included in older identifiers. These include Moldova, Belarus, Kazakhstan, Kyrgyzstan and Tajikistan, sometimes called "the post-Soviet Baltic republics."

There are also listings for the entirely bogus stamps of some entities, like Thomond, Nagaland, South Moluccas and Upper Yaffa, which never operated any postal service, but which are frequently encountered by beginning and intermediate-level collectors.

We don't suggest what you should collect, or how you should collect it. We do suggest, however, that an informed collector is one who will get the most out of the hobby. Helping collectors become informed is the purpose of this guide.

Is it a postage stamp?

The Scott catalog, like most other worldwide catalogs, lists adhesive postage stamps issued by national postal administrations to prepay national and international mail. The vast majority of the stamps that are cataloged have at least two characteristics in common: the name (or abbreviation of the name) of the country for which they were issued; and a number specifying the face value of the stamp. These characteristics have long been the minimum design requirements for stamps used by member-nations of the Universal Postal Union, the planet's oldest and arguably most successful international organization, which coordinates the movement of mail around the world.

Many stamps also have text or other letters or symbols indicating the currency in which the stamp is denominated, and/or showing that the function of the stamp is postal. However, with the decline in the use of adhesive revenue stamps in this century (which tended to be confused with postage stamps by some users, and still are by many collectors), many countries, including our own, have done away with these additional design elements.

A good many stamps, especially those issued prior to 1950, also may display an overprint of some kind. An overprint consists of additional text or numerals printed over a previously completed stamp. Overprints may change or confirm the face value of the stamp (in a special kind of overprint, called a surcharge), may indicate that a stamp has a special function, may alter the function it previously had, and may even show that the stamp is intended for use in another nation or place than the one printed on the underlying design.

When trying to identify an overprinted postage stamp, take note of the overprint first. When it comes to identifying a stamp, overprints usually take precedence over any other text that appears on it. Some of these more difficult-to-identify overprints appear on pages 126-30.

As with all rules, there are exceptions even to those laid down by the UPU. The stamps of Great Britain, for example, never display the name of the country. Ever since it issued the world's first postage stamp, the Penny Black, in 1840, Great Britain has incorporated the portrait, profile or silhouette of its reigning monarch into the design of its stamps.

Similarly, some stamps introduced before the UPU came into being don't indicate face value. Trinidad's red Britannia stamps of 1851-76, for example, display only the name of the island. Users at the time were expected to know that, because they were red, these stamps had a value of 1 penny.

Modern exceptions exist as well. For example, the kingdom of Saudi Arabia, which included the abbreviation "K.S.A." on most of its stamps of 1975-82, has for the last decade issued all-Arabic stamps that are best identified by an emblem of crossed swords beneath a palm tree.

A more widespread recent exception to the rule is the use of non-denominated postage stamps, not only by the United States, but also by Canada, Great Britain, France, Brazil, Poland and an ever-growing list of nations. These stamps allow issuing nations to prepare massive quantities of new stamps well before the rate changes for which they are required. Their lack of a specific denomination means they can be pressed into service when a new rate is declared, regardless of what the new rate turns out to be. On each of these non-denominated stamps, a letter (or "1st" and "2nd" on 1989-92 British definitives) correlates with a specific postal rate that is set shortly before the stamps are issued.

In theory, the use of non-denominated stamps is supposed to be restricted to internal or domestic mail from point to point within one country, which is not regulated by the UPU. In fact, however, such stamps do turn up on international mail, especially on mail between neighboring countries.

Stamps that aren't in the catalogs

A considerable number of stamps aren't listed in most worldwide stamp catalogs, generally because these stamps fail to meet one or more criteria. Either they aren't adhesive postage stamps, they aren't issued by national postal administrations, or they aren't capable of prepaying national and international mail.

Revenues: The one category that consistently causes the greatest confusion for stamp collectors is revenue stamps. Revenue stamps, which are also known as fiscals or tax stamps, are stamps issued to pay some government fee or service other than postage.

The United States alone has issued no fewer than 28 categories of revenue stamps as listed in the Scott U.S. specialized catalog, along with hundreds of state and municipal tax and taxpaid stamps that aren't listed in Scott. Most other nations that issued postage stamps from the 19th century to the mid-20th century issued their own revenue stamps, too, often in comparable profusion.

Revenue stamps are often very similar to their postal cousins in design, denomination, caliber and type of printing and general appearance. Almost all of them differ from postage stamps, however, in their inscriptions. If you have difficulty finding a stamp in a catalog, look for the inscription "Postage" (or its counterpart in the language of the issue, such as "Correos" in Spanish or "Postes" in French). If such an inscription appears on most or all of a country's postage stamps, but not on the stamp that you are attempting to identify, the stamp may well be a revenue.

Adhesive revenue stamps have been around since 1725. They are every bit as fascinating and collectible as postage stamps, although you won't find them listed in most postage stamp catalogs. Like postage stamps, most revenues are common and worth only a few pennies, but some are rare and valuable.

Local stamps: Stamps issued by private firms or regional authorities for use on municipal, local or regional mail are not listed in Scott or any other general postage stamp catalog because they are not considered to be general issues. Their use is usually much more limited, and because they are not subject to the same kinds of controls as nationally issued stamps, some of them have occasionally been manipulated (or made up altogether) to bilk collectors.

Local stamps can most often be recognized as such from their inscriptions, which rarely give the name of their country of origin. Usually the city, province or district in which they were to be used, or the firm that issued them, is listed instead.

As with revenues, most locals are fairly inexpensive, though a few are scarce and expensive. Specialized one-country catalogs (such as the Scott U.S. specialized catalog) are generally the best references for the locals of the countries that they cover.

Postal stationery imprints: Many nations have printed or embossed non-adhesive stamp designs onto postal cards, stamped envelopes, aerograms, lettercards and other kinds of stationery intended for postal use. These items are collectively referred to as postal stationery.

Especially in the earlier decades of the stamp hobby, collectors frequently cut out these imprinted or embossed designs to fit them into their albums. Designs cut out at right angles, with a fairly generous and equal amount of paper on all sides of the imprint, are referred to as cut squares. Some collectors trimmed the imprints more closely, so that they resemble and are sometimes confused with adhesive stamps. Postage stamp and postal stationery imprint designs from some countries and periods are virtually identical, which makes the two still easier to confuse.

Stamplike designs on unusually thick, thin or colored papers are sometimes these postal stationery cutouts. Cut down to the edges of their printed design, most of these have very little collector value.

Essays and proofs: Prior to the production and issuance of a new postage stamp, there often are a number of steps that may give rise to items that resemble, closely or otherwise, the finished product but differ from it in one or more details.

Essays are models of stamps prepared before the design has been officially approved. Proofs are models of stamps prepared after a stamp has been officially approved.

Most essays are easy to differentiate from issued adhesive postage stamps. Some, however, prepared in the final stages prior to approval, from dies or even plates anticipating approval of the finished design, greatly resemble actual stamps.

Proofs may be taken at any point in the final preparation of an issued stamp: by an engraver testing his skill as he prepares the master die; by the platemakers, to assure that the design is consistent and flaw-free on the finished plate; by the printer, to check and select one or more colors for the finished design.

Towards the last steps in this process, the resulting proofs closely resemble the designs of the issued stamps. Indeed, though most proofs are printed on special papers that differ from those used to print the final stamps, some may be made on gummed, perforated paper. If these differ in any way from the actual issued stamps, they will generally be regarded as proofs instead.

Collectors should understand that proofs and essays are by no means inferior objects. Some are more valuable and more highly regarded by specialist collectors than the issued stamps they preceded.

However, proofs of some issued stamps, while collectible as such, can also be a great deal less valuable than the stamps they resemble. Unfortunately, such proofs have sometimes been altered by unscrupulous individuals who hope to pass them off as actual stamps.

The Scott *Specialized Catalogue of United States Stamps* lists and values proofs and essays of U.S. stamps, enabling informed collectors to be alert to such fraudulent manipulation. Regrettably, much less information exists for the proofs of stamps from many other countries.

Cinderellas: Last, and far from least, are cinderellas, which may be loosely defined as any object that is similar to but is not a postage stamp.

This category may include items as diverse as unissued postage stamps, phantom and fantasy issues, advertising and propaganda labels, Christmas, Easter and anti-tuberculosis seals, airmail and registration serial number adhesives and patriotic vignettes. Cinderellas can include stickers from wartime ration books, gummed life insurance premium or union dues payment stubs, publisher's clearance giveaway adhesives and supermarket redemption promotions.

It's a dauntingly broad field. However, upon closer inspection few cinderellas appear to be stamps. Most lack the denomination or country name, and few if any have an inscription that would tend to indicate that they are postally valid. (Unissued stamps are a dismaying but relatively seldom-encountered exception.)

The back of the book

You've checked carefully, and the stamp you're trying to find isn't a revenue, a local or a cinderella. In fact, it has a 1940 postmark — but you can't find it anywhere in the listing of that country's stamps issued from 1925 to 1940. What's the problem?

One possibility is that it is a back-of-the-book stamp, listed near the end of the relevant country's listings in the Scott catalog.

The main body of the listings for almost all the stamp-issuing entities in the Scott catalog consists of so-called regular issues — the standard definitive and commemorative postage stamp used most frequently to prepay postage.

However, there are many other equally valid categories of stamps. Scott also lists these stamps in sections following the main body of listings for regular issues. That's why stamps in these categories are often referred to as "back-of-the-book" issues.

Among the better known back-of-the-book categories are: semipostal stamps; airmail stamps; special delivery stamps; postage due stamps; stamps surcharged or overprinted for use in post offices abroad; and Official stamps. Literally scores of other categories exist as well.

If you're unable to locate a stamp in the regular listings in the Scott catalog or any other catalog, be sure to check these "back-of-the-book" listings, too.

If you're still stumped

If you've tried everything and you're still unable to identify a given stamp, try consulting other catalogs, especially any specialized catalogs devoted to the country of issue. These often contain information on specialized items too esoteric to be listed in the worldwide references. Specialist societies, many of which are listed in *Linn's World Stamp Almanac*, may also be able to give you the information or the reference you need.

If you've tried everything and nothing has worked, send a clear photocopy of the stamp on a black background with all relevant details to Linn's Collectors' Forum, Box 29, Sidney, OH 45365. If we can identify it — or if it stumps us, too — we may be able to publish your question in *Linn's* weekly Collectors' Forum column.

Alphabetical listing of stamp inscriptions

The purpose of this listing is to assist the stamp collector in identifying the country under which the stamp is listed in the Scott *Standard Postage Stamp Catalogue*. It is not intended to be a gazetteer, so only words that actually appear on a stamp are included. If the country name is in English on the stamp and the country is listed in the Scott catalog by that name, it is omitted. When the country's name is in italics in this listing, this indicates that it is listed in the Scott catalog. If the name of the country is not in italics, it is not listed by Scott. Where both uppercase and lowercase versions of the same wording appears on stamps, only one is shown. Similarly, variations in print style and use of accents or diacritical marks have largely been ignored.

An asterisk (*) denotes a country's native name. Overprints and surcharges that change the nationality of the stamp have been given special attention. The many others that do not change the nationality have been omitted.

Some commonly encountered labels and locals, not listed by Scott, have been included, along with some common terms denoting revenues and telegraph stamps.

Wording in parentheses may be present.

Greek and Cyrillic inscriptions and overprints are listed separately after the main listing. These are followed by Cyrillic, Greek, Hindi, Gujarati and Oriya alphabets.

- A -

A. - (monetary unit) - *Macao, Timor*

AALBORG BYPOST - *Denmark*, local post

AALESUND BYPOST - *Norway*, local post

AARHUS BYPOST - *Denmark*, local post

A.B. - overprint on Russia - *Far Eastern Republic*

ABASI - (monetary unit) - *Afghanistan*

ABYSSINIA - *Ethiopia*

A.C.C.P. - *Azerbaijan*

AÇORES - alone or as overprint on stamps of Portugal - *Azores* (see Portugal also)

A.E.F. - on stamp inscribed "CENTENAIRE DU GABON" - *French Equatorial Africa*
- overprint on French postage due with overprint "Moyen-Congo" - *Middle Congo*

AEREO-TARG: POSNAN 1921 - *Poland*, semiofficial airmail

AEROPORT INTERNATIONAL DE KANDAHAR - *Afghanistan*

AEROVIVAS NACIONALES - *Puerto Rico*, semiofficial airmail

AFARS ET DES ISSAS - *Afars and Issas*

AFF EXCEP FAUTE TIMB - overprint on stamps of Ethiopia - *Ethiopia*

AFFRANCHᵀˢ POSTES - *France*, precancel

AFGHAN, AFGHANES - *Afghanistan*

AFRICA CORREIOS - *Portuguese Africa*

AFRICA OCCIDENTAL ESPAÑOLA* - *Spanish West Africa*

AFRICA ORIENTALE ITALIANA* - *Italian East Africa*

1

AFRIQUE EQU^(ALE) **FR**^(CAISE) - *French Equatorial Africa*

AFRIQUE EQUATORIALE (FRANÇAISE) - *French Equatorial Africa*

AFRIQUE EQUATORIALE FRANÇAISE - overprint on stamps of Gabon (no bars) - *Gabon*
- overprint (no bars) on stamps of Middle Congo - *Middle Congo* (with overprint "Tchad" - *Chad*)
- overprint with bars on stamps of Middle Congo or Gabon - *French Equatorial Africa*
- overprint on stamps of Ubangi - Shari - *Ubangi - Shari*

AFRIQUE EQUATORIALE GABON - *Gabon*

AFRIQUE FRANÇAISE LIBRE - alone or as overprint on stamps of French Equatorial Africa or Middle Congo - *French Equatorial Africa*

AFRIQUE OCCIDENTALE FRANÇAISE or **AFRIQUE OCCale FRçaise**
- *French West Africa*
- with **"SOUDAN"** - *French Sudan*

AFS - (monetary unit) - *Afghanistan*

AGUINALDO - *Philippines*, local revolutionary issue

A.H.P.D. - overprint on Azores - *Azores*, for use in Angra, Horta and Ponta Delgado

AIRMAIL - on stamp with Japanese characters - *Ryukyu Islands*

AITUTAKI - overprint on New Zealand or Cook Islands - *Aitutaki*

AJMAN STATE - not legitimate ("Ajman" alone is legitimate)

AJRORE - *Albania* airmail

ALAND - *Finland*, Aland Islands

ALAOUITES - overprint on stamps of France or Syria - *Alaouites*

ALBANIA - overprint on stamps of Italy - *Italy*, Offices in Turkey (Albania)

ALBANIE CENTRALE - 1915 issues for *Central Albania* (listed by Minkus)

ALDERNEY - *Great Britain*, Channel Islands (Some are unlisted locals.)

ALERTA - manuscript overprint on Peru - *Peru*, Ancachs

ALEXANDRIE - alone or as overprint on stamps of France - *France*, Offices in Egypt, Alexandria

ALGERIE* - alone or as overprint on stamps of France - *Algeria*

ALLEMAGNE DUITSCHLAND - overprint on stamps of Belgium - *Germany*, Belgian occupation

ALLENSTEIN - overprint on stamps of Germany - *Allenstein*

ALMAGUER - *Colombia*, fake postmaster's provisional

A.M.G.-F.T.T. or **AMG-FTT** - overprint on stamps of Italy - *Italy*, Trieste, Allied occupation

A.M.G.-V.G. - overprint on stamps of Italy - *Italy*, Venezia Giulia, Allied occupation

AMOY - *China*, treaty port local

A.M. POST DEUTSCHLAND - *Germany*, Allied occupation

AMSTERDAO - with "Portugal" overprint - *Portugal* postal tax

AMTLICHER VERKEHR - *German States*, Wurttemberg

ANDORRA - overprint on stamps of Spain - *Andorra*, Spanish administration

ANDORRE - alone or as overprint on stamps of France - *Andorra*, French administration

ANNA(S) - (monetary unit) - Aden, Bahrain, British East Africa, Burma,

India, Indian States, Iraq, Kuwait, Mesopotamia, Oman (Muscat), Pakistan, Somaliland Protectorate, Zanzibar

- overprint on stamps of France - *France*, Offices in Zanzibar
- overprint on stamps of Great Britain - *Oman* (Muscat)
- surcharge on stamps of Japan - *Burma*, Japanese occupation
- overprint on stamps of Turkey - *Mesopotamia*

ANTANANARIVO - *Madagascar* (British)

ANTARCTICA 1954 EXPEDITION - *Australia*, souvenir labels

ANTIOQUIA - *Colombia*, Antioquia Department

A.O. - overprint on Belgian Congo semipostal - *German East Africa*, Belgian occupation

AOF - overprint on stamps of France - *French West Africa*

A.O.I. - overprint on Italy postage due - *Italian East Africa*

A PAYER TE BETALEN - *Belgium, Belgian Congo* or *Ruanda-Urundi*, postage due

A PERÇEVOIR - *Belgium, Canada, France, Monaco* and many French colonies, postage due

- with "PERSE" - Iran, unissued postage due

APORTACION VOLUNTARIA - *Spain*, charity labels

APURIMAC - *Peru*, Apurimac

A.R. or **AR** - *Chile, Colombia, Montenegro, Panama*, acknowledgment of receipt

ARABIE S(A)OUDITE - *Saudi Arabia*

ARCHIPEL DES COMORES - *Comoro Islands*

A.R.COLON COLOMBIA - handstamp overprint on stamps of Colombia - *Panama*,
acknowledgement of receipt

A RECEBER - *Portugal* and colonies, postage due

ARCOUDI - bogus issue

ARENDAL BYPOST - *Norway*, local post

AREQUIPA - *Peru*, Arequipa

ARIARY - *Madagascar*, local issue

ARMENWET - overprint on stamps of the Netherlands - *Netherlands*, officials

ASCENSION - overprint on stamps of St. Helena - *Ascension*

ASSISTENCIA D.L. No. 72 - overprint on war tax stamp of Portuguese India - *Timor*

ASSISTENCIA NATIONAL AOS TUBERCULOSOS - *Portugal*, franchise stamp

ASSOBLA - overprint on stamps of Spanish Guinea - *Spanish Guinea*, for use in Elobey, Annabon and Corisco

A-T or **A&T** - overprint on stamps of French Colonies - *Annam & Tonkin*

ATT(S) - (monetary unit) - *Thailand*

AUNUS - overprint on stamps of Finland - *Russia*, Finnish occupation

AUR. - (monetary unit - Aurar) - *Iceland*

AUSSERKURS - overprint on stamps of Switzerland - demonetized stamps

AUSTRALIAN ANTARCTIC TERRITORY - *Australia*

AUST. SIGILLUM NOV. CAMB. - *New South Wales*

AUTOPAKETTI - *Finland*, parcel post

3

AVION MESSRE TAFARI - *Ethiopia*

AVISPORTO - *Denmark*, newspaper stamp

AVO(S) - (monetary unit) - Macao, Timor

AYACUCHO - *Peru*, Ayacucho provisional

AYUNTAMIENTO DE BARCELONA - *Spain* postal tax, delisted by Scott

AZAD HIND - stamps prepared by Nazi Germany for use in India, but never issued

AZERBAIDJAN - *Azerbaijan*

AZIRBAYEDJAN - overprint on Russia - Azerbaijan, private overprint

- **B** -

B - overprint on Straits Settlements - *Bangkok* (British) - in oval, no country name - Belgium parcel post

B. or **B.Dpto.Zelaya** - overprint on stamps of Nicaragua - *Nicaragua*, Zelaya Province

BADEN - *German States*, Baden - also *Germany*, Baden, under French occupation

B.A.ERITREA - overprint on stamps of Great Britain - *Great Britain*, Offices in Eritrea

BAGAGES REISGOED - overprint on stamps of Belgium parcel post - *Belgium*, revenue

BAGHDAD IN BRITISH OCCUPATION - overprint on stamps of Turkey - *Mesopotamia*, British occupation

BAHA 1943 - surcharge on stamps of Philippines, Japanese occupation

BAHAWALPUR - *Pakistan*, Bahawalpur State

BAHRAIN - overprint on stamps of India or Great Britain - *Bahrain*

BAHT - (monetary unit) - *Thailand*

BAI - (monetary unit) - *Italian States*, Romagna

BAJ - (monetary unit - Bajocchi) - *Italian States*, Roman States

BAJAR PORTO - alone or as overprint on stamps of Netherlands Indies - *Indonesia* postage due

BAMRA - *India*, Bamra native state

BANAT BACSKA - overprint on stamps of Hungary - *Hungary*, Serbian occupation

BANI - (monetary unit) - alone or as overprint on stamps of Germany or Austria - *Romania*, German or Austrian occupation
- overprint on stamps of Hungary - *Hungary*, Romanian occupation

BARANYA - overprint on stamps of Hungary - *Hungary*, Serbian occupation

BARBUDA - overprint on stamps of Antigua or Leeward Islands - *Barbuda*

BARCELONA - *Spain* (Barcelona issued many local stamps)

BARDSEY - Great Britain, publicity label

BARRANQUILLA - with "Franqueo Particular" - *Colombia*, private local

BARWANI - *India*, Barwani feudatory state

BASEL - *Switzerland*, Basel canton

B.A. SOMALIA - overprint on stamps of Great Britain - *Great Britain*, Offices in Somalia

BASUTOLAND - alone or as overprint on stamps of South Africa -

Basutoland

BATAVIA - *Netherlands Indies,* postage due

BATEKEN - phantom issue

B.A.TRIPOLITANIA - overprint on stamps of Great Britain - *Great Britain,* Offices in Tripolitania

BAYAR PORTO - *Indonesia,* postage due

BAYERN* - or **BAYER. POSTAZE** - *German States,* Bavaria

BAYER. STAATSEISENB. - *Bavaria,* railway issues

B.C.A. - overprint on stamps of Rhodesia - *British Central Africa*

B.C.G. - *Dominican Republic,* postal tax

B.C.M. - *Madagascar,* British consular mail

B.C.O.F. JAPAN 1946 - overprint on stamps of Australia - *Australia,* military stamps

BECHUANALAND - overprint on stamps of South Africa - *Bechuanaland Protectorate*

BECHUANALAND PROTECTORATE - alone or as overprint on stamps of Great Britain or Cape of Good Hope - *Bechuanaland Protectorate*

BELALP - *Switzerland,* hotel post

BELARUS - formerly Byelorussia

BELGIE, BELGIQUE* - *Belgium*

BELGIEN - overprint on stamps of Germany - *Belgium,* German occupation

BELGISCH CONGO* - *Belgian Congo*

BELIZE - alone or as overprint on stamps of British Honduras - *Belize*

BENADIR - *Somalia* (Italian Somaliland)

BENGASI - overprint on stamps of Italy - *Italy,* Offices in Africa

BENIN - alone or as overprint on stamps of Dahomey or French Colonies - *Benin*

BEPPU - only English inscription on stamp - *Japan*

BEQUIA - *St. Vincent Grenadines,* Bequia Island

BERGEDORF - *German States,* Bergedorf

BERGENS BYPOST - *Norway,* local post

BERLIN - alone or as overprint on stamps of Germany - *Germany,* Berlin (East or West)
- **STADT BERLIN** is Soviet Zone

BERNERA ISLANDS - Scotland, publicity label

BESA - (monetary unit) - *Somalia* - overprint on stamps of Albania (translates genuine)

BESETZTES GEBIET NORDFRANKREICH - overprint on stamps of France covering two stamps - *France,* German occupation

BHOPAL STATE or BHOPAL GOVT. - *India,* Bhopal feudatory state

BHOR - *India,* Bhor feudatory state

BIAFRA - alone or as overprint on stamps of Nigeria - *Nigeria,* revolutionary issues (not listed by Scott)

BICENTENARIO DE TALCA - *Chile,* Talca postal tax

BIE - overprint on stamps of Switzerland - *Switzerland,* Official for International Bureau of Education

BIJAWAR - *India,* Bijawar feudatory state

BILPAKET - *Finland* parcel post

B.I.O.T. - overprint on stamps of Seychelles - *British Indian Ocean*

Territory

BIRR - (monetary unit) - *Ethiopia*

B L C I - (one letter in each corner) - *India*, Bhopal feudatory state

B.M.A. ERITREA - overprint on stamps of Great Britain - *Great Britain*, Offices in Eritrea

BMA MALAYA - overprint on stamps of Straits Settlements - *Straits Settlements*

B.M.A. SOMALIA - overprint on stamps of Great Britain - *Great Britain*, Offices in Somalia

B.M.A. TRIPOLITANIA - overprint on stamps of Great Britain - *Great Britain*, Offices in Tripolitania

B.N.F. CASTELLORIZO - overprint on stamps of France, Offices in Turkey - *Castellorizo*, French occupation

BOGACH(ES), BOGCHAH, BOGSHAS - (monetary unit) - *Yemen*

BOGOTA - *Colombia*, local for city of Bogota

BÖHMEN UND (or u.) MÄHREN - *Czechoslovakia*, Bohemia and Moravia

BOLIVAR - *Colombia*, Bolivar Department

BOLIVIANA - *Bolivia*

BOLLA DELLA POSTA DI SICILIA - *Italian States*, Two Sicilies

BOLLA DELLA POSTA NAPOLETANA - *Italian States*, Two Sicilies

BOLLETTA - *San Marino* parcel post

BOLLO POSTALE - *San Marino*

BOLLO STRAORDINARIO PER LE POSTE - *Italian States*, Tuscany

BOPHUTHATSWANA - *South Africa*, native homeland

BOSNIA i HERCEGOVINA - overprint on stamps of Bosnia and Herzegovina - *Yugoslavia*, issues for Bosnia and Herzegovina

BOSNIEN HERZEGOWINA or **HERCEGOVINA*** - *Bosnia and Herzegovina*

BOUVET OVA - overprint on stamps of Norway - not recognized as official

BOYACA - *Colombia*, Department of Boyaca

BRAPEX - *Brazil*

BRASIL - *Brazil*

BRAUNSCHWEIG - *German States*, Brunswick

BRECHOU - *Guernsey* local issues

BREMEN - *German States*, Bremen

BRIEFPOST - *Germany*, French occupation

BRITISH BECHUANALAND - alone or as overprint on stamps of Cape of Good Hope or Great Britain - *Bechuanaland* (British)

BRITISH CONSULAR MAIL ANTANANARIVO - overprint on stamps of India or Zanzibar - *British East Africa*

BRITISH EAST AFRICA COMPANY - overprint on stamps of Great Britain - *British East Africa*

BRITISH NEW GUINEA - *Papua New Guinea*

BRITISH NORTH BORNEO - *North Borneo*

BRITISH OCCUPATION - overprint on stamps of Russia or Batum - *Batum*

BRITISH PROTECTORATE OIL RIVERS - overprint on stamps of Great Britain - *Niger Coast Protectorate*

BRITISH SOMALILAND - overprint on stamps of India - *Somaliland Protectorate*

BRITISH SOUTH AFRICA COMPANY - alone or as overprint on stamps of Cape of Good Hope - *Rhodesia* (British South Africa)

BRITISH VICE CONSULATE ANTANANARIVO - *Madagascar* (British)

BRITISH (or **BR.**) **VIRGIN ISLANDS** - *Virgin Islands*

BRUNEI - alone or as overprint on stamps of Labuan - *Brunei*

BRUSSEL or **BRUXELLES** - *Belgium*

BUCHANAN - with "Registered," no country name - *Liberia*

BUENOS AIRES - *Argentina*, Buenos Aires Province

BULGARIE* - *Bulgaria*

BUNDESREPUBLIK DEUTSCHLAND* - *Germany, Federal Republic*

BUNDESLAND SACHSEN - *Germany*, Soviet Zone, Saxony

BUNDI - *India*, Bundi feudatory state

BURGENLAND - *Austria*, provincial tax stamp

BURKINA FASO* - formerly Upper Volta

BURMA - alone or as overprint on stamps of India - *Burma*

BUSHIRE - overprint on stamps of Iran - *Bushire*, British occupation

BUSSAHIR - *India*, Bussahir feudatory state

BUSSPAKET - *Finland* parcel post

BUU-CHINH - *Vietnam*

- C -

C - overprint on stamps of Paraguay - *Paraguay*, Interior Office

C1HS in circle - handstamp on stamps of Germany - *Upper Silesia*

CABO - overprint on stamps of Nicaragua - *Nicaragua*, Cabo Gracias a Dios

CABO DELGADO - *Nyassa*, unissued stamp

CABO JUBI - overprint on stamps of Rio De Oro - *Cape Juby*

CABO JUBY*, **CABO-JUBY** - overprint on stamps of Spain or Spanish Morocco - *Cape Juby*

CABO VERDE* - alone or as overprint on stamps of Portuguese Africa - *Cape Verde*

CACHES or **CA** - (monetary unit) - overprint on France or French Colonies postage due - *French India*
postage due

CALCHI - overprint on stamps of Italy - *Italy*, Aegean Islands - Calchi

CALF OF MAN - Great Britain, publicity labels

CALIMNO or **CALINO** - overprint on stamps of Italy - *Italy*, Aegean Islands - Calino

CALLAO - overprint on stamps of Chile - *Peru*, Chilean occupation

CALVE ISLAND, SCOTLAND - publicity labels

CAMB AUST SIGILLUM NOV - (motto on seal) - *New South Wales*

CAMBODGE* - *Cambodia*

CAMEROON - English spelling of *Cameroun*

CAMEROONS U.K.T.T. - overprint on stamps of Nigeria - *Cameroons*, British trust territory

CAMEROUN - alone or as overprint on stamps of Middle Congo or Gabon - *Cameroun*

CAMPECHE - *Mexico*, provisional issue of Campeche State

CAMPIONARIA DI TRIPOLI - on stamps with "Poste Italiane" - *Libya*

CAMPIONE D'ITALIA - Italian enclave in Switzerland that issued stamps in 1944-1952

CANAL MARITIME DE SUEZ - Suez Canal Company locals

CANAL ZONE - overprint on stamps of Colombia, Panama or U.S. - *Canal Zone*, U.S.

CANARIAS - overprint on stamps of Spain - *Spain*, Canary Islands

CANEA (LA) - overprint on stamps of Italy - *Italy*, Offices in Crete

CANNA (EILEEN CHANAIDH) - publicity label

CANOUAN ISLAND - *St. Vincent Grenadines*

CANTON - overprint on stamps of Indochina - *France*, Offices in China

CARCHI - overprint on stamps of Italy - *Italy*, Aegean Islands - Calchi

CARITAS - Belgium, Denmark, Luxembourg - semipostal

CARN IAR - unissued local, overprinted for private London delivery service

CARUPANO - *Venezuela*, Carupano local

CARTILLA POSTAL DE ESPANA - *Spain*, franchise stamp

CASH - (monetary unit) - *India* - Travancore

CASO - overprint on stamps of Italy - *Italy*, Aegean Islands - Caso

CASTELLORISO or **CASTELLORIZO** - overprint on stamps of France - *Castellorizo*, French occupation

CASTELROSSO - alone or as overprint on stamps of Italy - *Castellorizo*

CATALUNA - *Spain*, Carlist stamp

CAUCA - *Colombia*, Cauca Department

CAVALLE - alone or as overprint on stamps of France - *France*, Offices in Turkey   (see Greece - Cavala also)

CCCP - *Russia*

C.CH. (with "5") - overprint on stamps of French Colonies - *Cochin China*

C. (or Cs) DE PESOS - (monetary unit) - *Philippines*

ČECHY A MORAVA - *Czechoslovakia*, Bohemia and Moravia

C.E.F. - overprint on stamps of German Cameroun - *Cameroons*, British occupation

CEFALONIA e ITACA - overprint on stamps of Greece - *Ionian Islands*, Italian occupation

CENT(S) - (monetary unit) - overprint on stamps of Germany - *France*, German occupation
- overprint with crown on stamps of India - *Straits Settlements*
- overprint on stamps of Russia - *Russia*, Offices in China
- surcharge on stamps of Japan - *Burma*, Japanese occupation

CENTENAIRE ALGERIE - *France*

CENTENAIRE DE L'ALGERIE - *Algeria*

CENTENAIRE DU GABON - *French Equatorial Africa*

CENTESIMI - (monetary unit) - alone - Italy, Italian Colonies (Cyrenaica, Eritrea, Libya, Oltre Guiba, Somalia), San Marino, Vatican, Uruguay, Venezuela
- overprint on stamps of Austria or Bosnia - *Italy*, Austrian occupation

CENTESIMI DI CORONA - (monetary unit) - overprint in sans-serif letters on stamps of Italy - *Dalmatia*
- overprint in serif letters on stamps of Italy - *Austria*, Italian occupation

Alphabetical listing of stamp inscriptions

CENTIMES - (monetary unit) - Belgium, France, Liechtenstein, Luxembourg, Haiti, etc.
- overprint on stamps of Austria - *Austria*, Offices in Crete
- overprint on stamps of Germany - *Germany*, Offices in Turkey

CENTIMES à PERCEVOIR - France, French Colonies or Monaco postage due
- with numeral, no country name - *Guadeloupe* postage due

CENTIMOS - (monetary unit) - Cuba, Philippines, Spain, Venezuela and others
- surcharge on stamps of France - *French Morocco*

CENT PO FE - (monetary unit) - *Philippines*

CENTRAFRICAIN(E) - *Central Africa*

CENTRAL AMERICAN STEAMSHIP CO. - bogus labels

CERIGO - Italian overprint on stamps of Greece - Ionian Islands, bogus issue

CESKOSLOVENSKA - overprint on stamps of Austria or Hungary - *Czechoslovakia* semipostal

CESKOSLOVENSKA REPUBLIKA - overprint on stamps of Austria - private issue

CESKO SLOVENSKA (STATNI) POSTA - overprint on stamps of Austria or Hungary - unofficial issues

CESKOSLOVENSKE VOJSKO NA RUSI - Czechoslovak Legion in Siberia

CESKOSLOVENSKO(A)* - *Czechoslovakia*

CESKO SLOVENSKY STAT - overprint on stamps of Austria - private issue

CFA - overprint on stamps of France - *France*, Reunion

C.G.H.S. - overprint on stamps of Germany - *Upper Silesia*, Official

CH - (Followed by Oriental characters) - *Korea*

CHAHI(S) - (monetary unit) - *Iran*

CHALA - overprint on stamps of Peru - *Peru*, Chala provisional

CHAMBA - *India*, Chamba State

CHANCELLERIE - *Iran* overprint changed postage to fiscal or revenue stamps

CHARKHARI - *India*, Charkhari State

CHEFOO - *China*, Chee Foo local post

CHEMINS DE FER (SPOORWEGEN) - *Belgium*, parcel post

CHIFFRE TAXE - on perforated stamps with no country name - *France* postage due
- on imperforate stamps - *France* or *French Colonies*, postage due
- denominated in para or piastre - *Turkey*, postage due
- with "RH" - *Haiti*

CHIHUAHUA - *Mexico*, Chihuahua provisional

CHINA, CHINESE EMPIRE or **CHINESE IMPERIAL POST** - *Republic of China*

CHINA - overprint on stamps of Germany - *Germany*, Offices in China or Kiauchau
- overprint on stamps of Hong Kong - *Great Britain*, Offices in China

CHINE - overprint on stamps of France or Indochina - *France*, Offices in China

CHINKIANG - *China,* treaty port local post

CHOKINKYOFU - *Indonesia* savings stamp, Japanese occupation

CHORRILLOS LIMA CALLAO - *Peru*

CHRISTIANSSUNDS (or **CHR.SUNDS**) **BYPOST** - *Norway* local post

CHRISTMAS ISLAND - overprint on stamps of Australia - *Christmas Island*

CHUNGKING L.P.O. - *China,* Treaty Port local

CILICIE - overprint on stamps of France or Turkey - *Cilicia*

CINQUANTENAIRE 24 SEPTEMBRE 1852 1903 - overprint with eagle on French Colonies postage due - *New Caledonia* postage due

CIRENAICA - alone or as overprint on stamps of Italy or Tripolitania - *Cyrenaica*

CIRCUITO DELLE OASI/ TRIPOLI/ MAGGIO-1934-XII - overprint on stamps of Libya - *Tripolitania*

CISKEI - *South Africa,* Ciskei native homeland

CLIPPERTON - overprint on stamps of Mexico - doubtful validity

CLIPPERTON ISLAND - local post

C.M.T. in box - overprint on stamps of Austria - *Western Ukraine,* Romanian occupation

CN - (monetary unit) - *Korea*

COAMO - *Puerto Rico,* U.S. administration

COCHIN (ANCHAL) - *India,* Cochin feudatory state (see Cochin China also)

Co.Ci. - overprint on stamps of Yugoslavia - *Yugoslavia,* Llubljana - Italian occupation

COLIS POSTAL or **POSTAUX** - Belgium, St. Pierre & Miquelon or Tunisia parcel post
- overprint on stamps of Dahomey - *Dahomey* parcel post
- overprint on stamps of French Colonies, with "Cote d'Ivoire" - *Ivory Coast,* parcel post

COLOMBIA - with map of Panama, "Antillas" and "Pacifico" - *Panama*

COLONIA DE MOÇAMBIQUE - *Mozambique*

COLONIA DE RIO DE ORO - *Rio De Oro*

COLONIA ERITREA - overprint on stamps of Italy - *Eritrea*

COLONIALE (or **COLONIE**) **ITALIANE** - alone or as overprint on stamps of Italy - *Italian Colonies*

COLONIES DE L'EMPIRE FRANÇAISE - *French Colonies*

COLONIES POSTES - *French Colonies*
- with surcharge - Cochin China, Diego Suarez, Gabon, Madagascar,
Nossi Be, New Caledonia, Reunion, Senegal or Tahiti

COMITE FRANÇAISE DE LA LIBERATION NATIONALE - *French Colonies,* semipostal

COMMISSION DE CONTROIE PROVISOIRE - *Albania*

COMMISSION DE GOUVERNEMENT HAUTE SILESIE - *Upper Silesia*

COMMISSION INTERALLIEE MARIENWERDER - alone or as overprint on stamps of Germany - *Marienwerder*

COMMUNICACIONES - *Spain*

COMORES - *Comoro Islands*

COMP^A (or **COMPANHIA**) **DE MOÇAMBIQUE** - alone or as overprint on stamps of Mozambique - *Mozambique Company*

COMPANHIA DO NYASSA - *Nyassa* (Portuguese)

COMPANIA COLOMBIANA DE NAVEGACION AEREA - *Colombia* airmail

COMUNE DI CAMPIONE - Italy local issue

CONDOMINIUM DES NOUVELLES HEBRIDES - *New Hebrides*, French issue

CONDOMINIUM NEW HEBRIDES - *New Hebrides*, British issue

CONDOR - on Brazil - *Brazil*, private airmail carrier

CONFED. GRANADINA - *Colombia*, Granadine Confederation

CONFOEDERATIO HELVETICA - *Switzerland*

CONGO - alone or as overprint on stamps of Belgian Congo - *Congo Democratic Republic*
   - with "Republique Du" - *Congo Democratic Republic* or *Congo People's Republic*
   - overprint on stamps of Angola or with "Portugal," "Portuguesa" or "Republica" - *Portuguese Congo*
   - with "Democratique" - *Congo Democratic Republic*
   - with "Populaire" - *Congo People's Republic*

CONGO BELGE - *Belgian Congo*

CONGO FRANÇAIS - alone or as overprint on stamps of French Colonies - *French Congo*

CONGO FRANÇAIS GABON - *Gabon*

CONGRESO DE LOS DIPUTADOS - *Spain*, Official

CONGRESO INTERNACIONAL DE FERROCARRILES - *Spain*

CONSTANTINOPLE - overprint on stamps of Russia - *Russia*, Offices in Turkey

CONSTANTINOPOLI - overprint on stamps of Italy - *Italy*, Offices in Turkey

CONTRAMARCA - *Ecuador*, control overprint

CONTRIBUIDAO INDUSTRIAL ULTRAMAR - *Macao*

COO - overprint on stamps of Italy - *Italy*, Aegean Islands - Coo

COOK ISLANDS (or **I.S.DS.**) - overprint on stamps of New Zealand - *Cook Islands*

COOK ISLANDS with **NIUE** - *Niue*

CORDOBA - *Argentina*, Cordoba Province

COREA(N) or **COREE** - *Korea*

CORFU - overprint on stamps of Greece or Italy - *Corfu*

COROCO - publicity label

CORONA - (monetary unit) - overprint on stamps of Italy - *Austria*, Italian occupation or *Dalmatia*

CORREIO(S) - Brazil, Portugal or Portuguese colonies
   - with "Bateken" - phantom issue

CORREIOS E TELEGRAPHOS - *Portugal*

CORREIOS MULTA - *Portugal*

CORREO AEREO - with no country name - *Spain*

CORREO CERTdo, CERTIFO or **CERTIFICADO** - *Spain*

CORREO DE LOS EE UU DE VEEZA - *Venezuela*

CORREO ESPAÑOL MARRUECOS - overprint on stamps of Spain - *Spanish Morocco*

CORREO ESPAÑOL TANGER - overprint on stamps of Spain - *Spanish Morocco*, Tangiers

CORREO SUBMARINO - *Spain*, 1938 submarine voyage

CORREO URBANO DE BOGOTA - *Colombia*, city of Bogota

CORREO URGENTE - *Spain*, special delivery

CORREOS - with no country name - Colombia, Cuba, Dominican Republic, Peru, Philippines, Spain, Uruguay
- also appears on Latin American countries, Philippines and Spain

CORREOS 1854Y55 - *Philippines*

CORREOS ARGENTINOS - *Argentina*

CORREOS (DE) ESPAÑA - *Spain*

CORREOS FRANCO - *Spain*

CORREOS INTERIOR - *Philippines, Spain*

CORREOS NACIONALES (or **NALES**) - *Colombia*

CORREOS OAXACA - *Mexico*, Oaxaca

CORREOS URBANOS MEDELLIN - *Colombia*, local issue

CORREOS Y TELEGS (or **TELEG^{EOS}**) - *Spain*

CORREOS Y TELEGRAFOS - *Argentina*

CORESPONDENCIA URGENTE - *Spain* special delivery

CORRIENTES - *Argentina*, Corrientes Province

COS - overprint on stamps of Italy - *Italy*, Aegean Islands - Coo

"COSTA ATLANTICA" B. - overprint on stamps of Nicaragua - *Nicaragua*, Zelaya Province

"COSTA ATLANTICA" C. - overprint on stamps of Nicaragua - *Nicaragua*, Cabo Gracias A Dios

CôTE DES SOMALIS, CôTE FRANÇAISE (FRse) DES SOMALIS - *Somali Coast*

CôTE d'IVOIRE - alone or as overprint on stamps of Burkina Faso (Haute Volta) or French Colonies - *Ivory Coast*

COTTBUS - *Germany*, World War II local

COUNANI - bogus issues

CRETE - *France*, Offices in Crete

CREVICHON - *Great Britain*, local carriage label - Jethou

CROISSANT ROUGE TURC - *Turkey*

CRUZ ROJA DOMINICANA - *Dominican Republic*

CRUZ ROJA HONDURENE (or **HONDVRENA**) - *Honduras*

CRUZ VERMELHA PORTUGUESA - *Portugal*

CRVENI KRST - overprint on stamps of Yugoslavia, Offices Abroad - *Yugoslavia*, Offices Abroad semipostal

CRVENI KRST MONTENEGRO - overprint on stamps of Montenegro or Yugoslavia -
Montenegro

C.S. - *Confederate States of America*

C.S.A.R. - overprint on stamps of Transvaal - *Transvaal*, control mark for Central South African Railway

CT. or **CTOT** - (monetary unit) - *Bulgaria*

CUARTO(S) - (monetary unit) - *Philippines, Spain*

CUAUTLA - *Mexico*, Cuautla provisional issue

CUBA - overprint on stamps of United States - *Cuba*, U.S. administration

CUBA 1898 y 99 - With crown and coat of arms - *Cuba*, fiscal stamp

CUERNAVACA - *Mexico*, Cuernavaca provisional issue

CUNDINAMARCA - *Colombia*, Cundinamarca State

CURAÇAO - *Netherlands Antilles*

CUZCO - overprint on stamps of Peru or Arequipa, Peru - *Peru*, Cuzco provisional issue

C.X.C. - overprint on stamps of Bosnia and Herzegovina - *Yugoslavia*, issues for Bosnia and Herzegovina

CYPRUS - alone or as overprint on stamps of Great Britain - *Cyprus*

- **D** -

D - overprint on stamps of SCADTA semiofficial airmail of Colombia - indicated stamp was a Consular stamp sold in Denmark
- (for "Dinar") - (monetary unit)
- on stamps with Arabic writing - *Iran*
- white in black circle overprint on stamps of Netherlands Indies - *Netherlands Indies* Official

d - (for "pence") - (monetary unit) - preceded by a numeral on stamp with king or queen's head, but no country name - *Great Britain*

DAHLAK ISLANDS - *Ethiopia*, local stamps

DAHOMEY - *Dahomey* or *Benin*

DAI NIPPON - overprint on stamps of Straits Settlements or Malaya - *Malaya*, Japanese occupation

DANMARK* - *Denmark*

DANSK VESTINDIEN (or **VESTINDISKE**) - *Danish West Indies*

DANZIG - overprint on stamps of Germany - *Danzig*

DARDANELLES - overprint on stamps of Russia - *Russia*, Offices in Turkey

DATIA - *India*, Duttia feudatory state

DAVAAR - *Scotland*, bogus issue

D.B.L.(P) - in script - overprint on stamps of Russia or Siberia - *Far Eastern Republic*
- overprint on stamps of Russia with three-bar surcharge - *Siberia*

D.B.S.R. - Danube and Black Sea Railway local stamps

D. de A. PROVISIONAL - *Colombia*, Antioquia Department

DDR - *German Democratic Republic*

DÉDÉAGH - alone or as overprint on stamps of France - *France*, Offices in Turkey

DEFICIT - *Peru*, postage due

DELEGACOES - *Portugal*, franchise stamp

DE LEON - *Ecuador*, control overprint

DEL GOLFO DE GUINEA - *Spanish Guinea*

DENWAISEN SIROTAM - surcharge on stamps of Italy - *Yugoslavia*, German occupation of Llubljana

DERECHOS DE ENTREGA - *Spain*, delivery tax

DERECHOS DE FIRMA - *Philippines*, revenue (some with "Habillitado" overprint used for postage)

DETACHMENT U.S.A. - overprint on stamps of Belgian Congo - bogus

DEUTƒCHES REICH - *Germany* - overprint on stamps of Bavaria -

13

Bavaria
- overprint on stamps of Danzig - *Danzig*
- with "Bohmen u. Mahren" - *Czechoslovakia*, Bohemia and Moravia
DEUTSCHE BUNDESPOST - *Germany*, Federal Republic
- if inscribed "Berlin" - *Germany*, West Berlin
- if inscribed "Saarland" - *Saar*
DEUTSCHE DEMOKRATISCHE REPUBLIK* - *German Democratic Republic*
FELDPOST - *Germany*, military parcel post
FLUGPOST - *Germany*, airmail
LUFTPOST - *Germany*, airmail
MILITAER - VERWALTUNG MONTENEGRO - overprint on stamps of Yugoslavia - *Montenegro*, German occupation
NATIONAL VERSAMMLUNG - *Germany*
POST (or **POƒT**) - *Germany*, East (Soviet Zone - Western Saxony) , West or Berlin
POST OSTEN - overprint on stamps of Germany - *Poland*, German occupation
PRIVAT-POST - *Germany*, private local post
REICHSPOST - *Germany*
DEUTSCHES REICH - *Germany*
DEUTSCHES REICH GENERAL GOUVERNEMENT - *Poland*, German occupation
DEUTSCHLAND - *Germany*, Allied occupation
DEUTƒCHÖƒTERREICH - *Austria*
DEUTSCH NEU-GUINEA* - *German New Guinea*
   OSTAFRIKA* - *German East Africa*
   SÜDWESTAFRIKA* - *German Southwest Africa*
DHAR - *India*, Dhar State
DHUFAR - publicity label
DIEGO SUAREZ - overprint on stamps of French Colonies - *Diego Suarez*
DIENƒTMARKE - Bavaria, Danzig, Germany, Liechtenstein, Prussia, Saar Officials
DIENSTSACHE - *German States*, Wurttemberg or *Liechtenstein*, Official
DIENSTZEGEL - *Netherlands*
DILIGENCIA - *Uruguay*, early carrier issues
DINAR(S) - (monetary unit) - Algeria, Iran, Iraq, Jordan, Kuwait, Libya, South Arabia, Tunisia, United Arab Emirates, Yemen People's Democratic Republic, or Yugoslavia
DINERO - (monetary unit) - *Peru*
DIOS PATRIA LIBERTAD - on coat of arms - *Dominican Republic*
DIOS, PATRIA, REY - *Spain*, Carlist stamps
DISTRITO (with "18°") - overprint on stamps of Arequipa, Peru - *Peru*, Cuzco provisional
DISTRITO SUR DE LA BAJA CAL - *Mexico*
DJ or **DJIBOUTI** - overprint on stamps of Obock - *Somali Coast*
DJIBOUTI - (with **REPUBLIC DE**) - overprint on stamps of Afars and Issas - *Djibouti*
- (with **PROTECTORAT DE LA COTE DES SOMALIS**) - *Somali*

Coast
- on French common design airmail - *Somali Coast*

DM - overprint on stamps of Danzig - *Danzig*, Officials

DOLLAR - overprint on stamps of Russia - *Russia*, Offices in China

DOMINICANA REPUBLICA - *Dominican Republic*

DOPKATA or **DOPLATA** - *Central Lithuania* or *Poland* postage due

DOPLATIT or **DOPLATNE** - no country name - *Czechoslovakia*, postage due

DOUANE - revenue overprint on stamps of *South Africa*

DRACHMA - (monetary unit) - *Crete* and *Greece*

DRAGONERA - bogus issue

DRAKE'S ISLAND - *Great Britain*, private local issue

DRAMMEN BYPOST - *Norway* local

DRIJVENDE BRANDKAST - *Netherlands*, marine insurance

DRZ., DRZAVA, or **DRZAVNA** - alone or as overprint on stamps of Bosnia and Herzegovina - *Yugoslavia*

DRZAVNA - with **HRVATSKA** - *Croatia* or *Yugoslavia*

DUC. DI. PARMA - *Italian States*, Parma

DUE GRANA - *Italian States*, Two Sicilies

DUITSCH OOST AFRIKA BELGISCHE BEZETTING - overprint on stamps of Belgian Congo - *German East Africa*, Belgian occupation

DULCE ET DECORUM EST PRO PATRIA MORI - *Nepal*

DURAZZO - overprint on stamps of Italy - *Italy*, Offices in Turkey

DUTTIA - *India*, Duttia State

- **E** -

E - overprint on stamps of Bavaria - *German States*, Bavaria

EA - overprint on stamps of France - *Algeria*

E.A.F. - overprint on stamps of Great Britain - *Great Britain*, Offices in Africa - East Africa Forces

EAST AFRICA AND UGANDA PROTECTORATES - with portrait of King George V and watermark multiple crown and script CA - *Kenya, Uganda and Tanzania*
- with "G.E.A." overprint - *Tanganyika*
- otherwise - *East Africa and Uganda Protectorates*

EAST INDIA POSTAGE - *India* - if overprint with crown and new value - *Straits Settlements*

ECUADOR - overprint on stamps inscribed "Servicio De Transportes Aeros En Colombia" - *Ecuador* airmail

E.E.F. - *Palestine*, British occupation
- if stamp has Arabic overprint - *Jordan* - Transjordan

EESTE, EESTI*, or **ESTI** - *Estonia*

EESTI POST - overprint on stamps of Russia - *Estonia*

EE.UU.DE C.(or **COLOMBIA**) - *Colombia*

EE.UU.DE C.E.S.DEL T. - *Colombia*, Tolima Department

EGEO - overprint on stamps of Italy - *Italy*, Aegean Islands, general issue

EGYPTE or **EGYPTIENNES** - *Egypt*

EILMARKE - *Bosnia and Herzegovina*

EINZUZIEHEN - *Danzig*, postage due

EIRE* - *Ireland*

EIREANN - overprint on stamps of Great Britain - *Ireland*

EJERCITO RENOVADOR - *Mexico*, Sinaloa revolutionary issue

EL PARLAMENTO (ESPAÑOL) A CERVANTES - *Spain*, Official

EL SALVADOR* - *Salvador*

EL*f*A*f*s - overprint on stamps of Germany - *France*, German occupation of Alsace

ELUA KENETA - *Hawaii*

E MIRIDITIES - *Albania*, Unauthorized issue

EMPIRE CENTRAFRICAIN - *Central Africa*

EMPIRE D'ETHIOPIE - *Ethiopia*

EMPIRE FRANC (or FRANÇAISE) - *France or French Colonies*

EMP. OTTOMAN - *Turkey*
   - with "R.O." or "Roumelie Orientale" overprint - *Eastern Rumelia*
   - with crescent and Turkish inscription overprint - *Eastern Rumelia*
   (Some with additional overprint are *Turkey*)

EN - (monetary unit) - *Japan*

EP - characters that look like this on China or Japan indicate revenue stamp

EPMAKb - *South Russia*

EQUATEUR - *Ecuador*

ER - with Queen Elizabeth's head and no country name - *Great Britain*

E.R.I. - overprint on stamps of South Africa - *Transvaal*

ERITREA - overprint on stamps of Italy or Somalia - *Eritrea*
   - overprint on stamps of Great Britain - *Great Britain*, Offices in Africa - Eritrea

ERSTE K.K.pr.DONAU DAMPFSCHIFFFAHRT GESELLSHAFT - Danube Steam Navigation Co. mail service (private post)

ESCUELAS - *Venezuela*, revenue stamps, some of which were authorized for postage

E.S.DEL T. - *Colombia*, Tolima Department

ESPAÑA*or ESPAÑOLA - *Spain*

ESPAÑA SAHARA - *Spanish Sahara*

ESPAÑOL - *Spain*

ESPAÑOL GUAYANA - *Venezuela*, State of Guayana, local issues

ESTADO DA INDIA - *Portuguese India*

ESTADOS UNIDOS DE COLOMBIA - *Colombia*
   - with **E.S. de PANAMA** - *Panama*

ESTADOS UNIDOS DE NUEVA GRANADA - *Colombia*

EST AFRICAIN ALLEMAND OCCUPATION BELGE - overprint on stamps of Belgian Congo - *German East Africa*, Belgian occupation

ESTENSI - *Italian States*, Modena

ESTERO - overprint on stamps of Italy - *Italy*, Offices Abroad, general issue

ESTLAND EESTI - *Estonia*, German occupation

ETA - *Brazil*, private airmail carrier

ETABLISSEMENTS (or ETS.) (FRANÇAISE or FRANC.) DANS (or DE) L'INDÉ- *French India*

ETABLISSEMENTS DE L'OCEANIE - *French Polynesia*

ETAT AUTONOME DU SUD - KASAI - alone or as overprint on stamps of Congo - South Kasai, not recognized as a state

ETAT COMORIEN - *Comoro Islands*

ETAT DU CAMBODGE - *Cambodia*

ETAT DU CAMEROUN - *Cameroun*

ETAT FRANÇAIS - *France*

ETAT INDEPENDANT (or **IND.**) **DU CONGO** - *Belgian Congo*

ETHIOPIE or **ETHIOPIENNES** - *Ethiopia*

ETIOPIA - *Ethiopia*, Italian occupation

Eᵀˢ **FRANÇ**ˢ (or **FRANÇAIS**) **DE L'OCEANIE** - *French Polynesia*

E.U.DE COLOMBIA - *Colombia*

EUPEN or **EUPEN & MALMEDY** - overprint on stamps of Belgium - *Germany*, Belgian occupation

EXPED. SCIENT. - with oriental characters - *China*

EXPOSICION DE BARCELONA - *Spain*

    GENERAL ESPAÑOLA - *Spain*

    GRAL SEVILLA BARCELONA - *Spain*

EXPOSITION COLONIALE INTERNATIONALE PARIS 1931 - with no colony name - *France*

EXPOSITION INDUSTRIELLE DAMAS 1929 - *Syria*

EXPRESSO TOBON - *Colombia* local

EYNHALLOW - Scotland, bogus issue

- **F** -

F - (monetary unit) - surcharge on stamps of Germany - *France*, German occupation

    - overprint on SCADTA semiofficial airmail of Colombia - consular stamp sold in France

    - overprint on stamps of France - *France*, stamps supplied free to Spanish refugees in 1939

FACTAJ - overprint on stamps of Romania - *Romania*, parcel post

FA or **FANON** - (monetary unit) - surcharge on stamps of France or French Colonies - *French India*

FAO - *United Nations*, Food and Agriculture Organization

FALTPOST - *Finland*, military stamp

FARIDKOT - *India*, Faridkot State

FAUCONNIERE - *Great Britain*, local carriage label for Jethou

Fᵈᵒ· **POO.** - *Fernando Po*

FEDERACION VENEZOLANA - *Venezuela*

FEDERATED MALAY STATES - alone or as overprint on stamps inscribed "N. Sembilan" or "Perak" - *Malaya*

FEDERATED STATES OF MICRONESIA - *United States*, Trust Territory - Federated States of Micronesia

FEDERATION DU MALI - *Mali*

FEDERATION OF MALAYA - *Malaya*

FEDERATION OF SOUTH ARABIA - *South Arabia*, (British dependency)

FELDPOST - *Austria* or *Germany*, military stamps

FELKELO MAGYAROK ESZAKI HADSEREGE 1921 - overprint on

stamps of Hungary - Western Hungary (not listed by Scott)

FEN or **Fn** - (monetary unit) - Manchukuo or People's Republic of China - with "Poczta Polska" overprint - *Poland*

FERNANDO POO - *Fernando Po*

FEUDATORY STATE RAJ NANDGAM OP - *India*, Nandgaon State

FEZ-MEQUINEZ - *Morocco*, local post

FEZ-SEFRO - *Morocco*, local post

FEZZAN (GHADAMES) - *Libya*, French occupation

FEZZAN OCCUPATION FRANÇAISE - overprint on stamps of Italy or Libya - *Libya*, French occupation

F.G.N. - overprint on stamps of Nigeria - *Nigeria*, unissued Official

FIERA CAMPIONARIA DI TRIPOLI - on stamps inscribed "Poste Italiane"- *Libya*

FIERA DI TRIESTE - overprint on stamps of Italy - *Italy*, Trieste

FILIPᴬˢ or **FILIPINAS*** - *Philippines*

FILLER - (monetary unit) - *Hungary*

FIL(S) - (monetary unit) - Bahrain, Kuwait, South Arabia, United Arab Emirates

- on stamps with no country name - Iraq, Jordan (Transjordan) or Yemen People's Democratic Republic

FINSTERWALDE - *Germany*, World War II locals

FIUME - overprint on stamps of Hungary - *Fiume*

FIVME - *Fiume*

FLORIDA - *Uruguay*, airmail

FLÜCHTLINGSHILFE MONTENEGRO - overprint on stamps of Yugoslavia or Montenegro - *Montenegro*, German occupation semipostal

FLUGPOST - *Austria, Danzig, Germany* or *Memel*, airmail

F.N.F.L. - overprint on stamps of French Colonies - Free French Naval Forces

FOOCHOW - *China*, Foochow local post

FORCES FRANÇAISE LIBRES-LEVANT - alone or as overprint on stamps of Lebanon or Syria - *Syria*, Free French Administration

FORMOSA - appears with "China" on 1888 Formosa locals

FØROYAR - *Faroe Islands*

fr. - (monetary unit) - overprint with numeral on Senegal or Mauritania - *French West Africa*

FRANC. - *France*

FRANC - (monetary unit) - Belgium, France, French Andorra, French Colonies, Liechtenstein, Monaco, Switzerland

- overprint on stamps of Austria - *Austria*, Offices in Crete

FRANCA - overprint on stamps of Peru - *Peru*, Ancachs or Chiclayo

FRANÇAISE - *France* or *French Colonies*

- with overprint - *French Offices* in China, Egypt, Madagascar, Morocco, Turkish Empire or Zanzibar

FRANCE D'OUTRE-MER - *French Colonies*, general

FRANCHI POSTES - on *France*, precancel

FRANCISCO BERTRAND - *Honduras*

FRANCO - German States (Bremen), Philippines, Romania, Spain, Switzerland

FRANCO BOLLO - with no country name - if perforate - *Italy*

Alphabetical listing of stamp inscriptions

- if imperforate - *Italian States*, Sardinia or Two Sicilies
FRANCO BOLLO DI STATO - *Italy*, Official
FRANCO BOLLO POSTALE - on stamps with crossed keys - *Italian States*, Roman States
FRANCO BOLLO TOSCANO - *Italian States*, Tuscany
FRANCO MARKE - *German States*, Bremen
FRANCO SCRISOREI - *Romania*, Moldavia - Walachia
FRANK - (monetary unit) - *Albania*
FRANQUEO - over a coat of arms - *Peru*, Arequipa provisional
FRANQUEO (IMPRESOS) - *Spain*
FRANQUICIA POSTAL - *Spain*, franchise stamp
FRANZ JOSEPH LAND - 1872 North Pole Expedition labels
FREDERICA BYPOST - *Denmark*, local post
FREI DURCH ABLÖSUNG NR.16 - *Germany*, local Official for Baden
FREI DURCH ABLÖSUNG NR.21 - *Germany*, local Official for Prussia
FREIE STADT DANZIG - *Danzig*
FREIMARKE - with no country name - *German States*, Baden, Prussia, Thurn & Taxis or Wurttemberg
Freiftaat Bayern - overprint on stamps of Bavaria or Germany - *German States*, Bavaria
FRIMARKE, FRIMÆRKE or **FRM** - Danish West Indies, Denmark, Norway or Sweden
FRIMARKE LOKALBRIEF - *Sweden*, city postage
FRIMERKI - *Iceland*
FUERSTENTUM LIECHTENSTEIN - *Liechtenstein*

- G -

G - overprint on stamps of Cape of Good Hope - *Griqualand West*
- (monetary unit) - *Italian States*, Two Sicilies
GAB or **GABON** - overprint on stamps of French Colonies - *Gabon*
GAIRSEY, SCOTLAND - publicity label
GALAPAGOS - *Ecuador*, Galapagos Islands
GAMBIERS - overprint on stamps of French Colonies - unauthorized
G.& D.30 - overprint on stamps of French Colonies postage due - *Guadeloupe* postage due
GARCH - (monetary unit) - *Saudi Arabia*, Hejaz - Nejd
G.D. de LUXEMBOURG - *Luxembourg*
GD LIBAN - alone or as overprint on stamps of France - *Lebanon*
G.E.A. - overprint on stamps of East Africa & Uganda Protectorate - *German East Africa*, British occupation
- overprint on stamps of Kenya, Uganda and Tanganyika inscribed "East Africa and Uganda Protectorates" with script CA watermark - *Tanganyika*
GENERAL GOUVERNEMENT - *Poland*, German occupation
GENEVE - *Switzerland*, Canton of Geneva
GEN. GOUV. WARSCHAU - overprint on stamps of Germany - *Poland*, German occupation
GEORGIE or **GEORGIENNE** - *Georgia*
GERUSALEMME - overprint on stamps of Italy - *Italy*, Offices in Turkey

- Jerusalem

GHADAMES - *Libya*, French occupation

GHANA INDEPENDENCE 6th MARCH 1957 - overprint on stamps of Gold Coast - *Ghana*

GIBRALTAR - overprint on stamps of Bermuda - *Gibraltar*

GILBERT & ELLICE PROTECTORATE - overprint on stamps of Fiji - *Gilbert and Ellice Island*

GIORNALI STAMPE - *Italian States*, Sardinia, newspaper stamp

GNR - overprint on stamps of Italy - Republican National Guard issue for North Italy - considered to be locals

GOLFE DE BENIN - *Benin*

GOLFO DE GUINEA - alone or as overprint on stamps of Spain - *Spanish Guinea*

GORNY SLASK - *Upper Silesia*, Polish occupation - private issue

GOTEBORGS STADSPOST - *Sweden*, local post

GOVERNATORATO DEL MONTENEGRO - overprint on stamps of Yugoslavia - *Montenegro*, Italian administration

GOYA - *Spain*

GP.E. - overprint on stamps of French Colonies - *Guadeloupe*

GR - (monetary unit) - *Ukraine*

GR, GRA or **GRANA** - (monetary unit) - *Italian States*, Two Sicilies

GRAHAM LAND - overprint on stamps of Falkland Islands - *Falkland Islands*, Graham Land Dependency

GRANADA or **GRANADINA** - *Colombia*, Granadine Confederation

GRANDE COMORE - *Grand Comoro*

GRAND-DUCHE LUXEMBOURG - *Luxembourg*

GRAND LIBAN - alone or as overprint on stamps of France - *Lebanon*
- with "Syrie" - *Syria*

GREAT BARRIER ISLAND - *New Zealand* local

GRENADINES OF ST. VINCENT - *St. Vincent Grenadines*

GRENVILLE - on registry stamp with no country name - *Liberia*

G.R.I. - overprint on stamps of German New Guinea or Marshall Islands - *New Britain*
- overprint on stamps of German Samoa - *Samoa*, (British)

G.R.I.MAFIA - overprint on stamps of German East Africa or India - *German East Africa*, British occupation of Mafia (not listed by Scott)

GRIMSTAD BYPOST - *Norway*, local post

GRØNLAND - *Greenland*

GROSSDEUTSCHES REICH - *Germany* - with "Böhmen und Mähren" - *Czechoslovakia*, Bohemia and Moravia
- with "Generalgouvernement" - *Poland*, German occupation

GROSZY - (monetary unit) - *Poland*

GROTE - (monetary unit) - *German States*, Bremen

GROUCH - (monetary unit) - *Turkey*

GROUCHE - (monetary unit) - *Saudi Arabia*

GRUNAY - publicity label

GUADALAJARA - *Mexico*, Guadalajara provisional

GUADELOUPE - overprint on stamps of French Colonies - *Guadeloupe*

GUAM - overprint on stamps of the United States - *United States*, Guam

GUANACASTE - overprint on stamps of Costa Rica - *Costa Rica*,

Guanacaste Province

GUAYANA - *Venezuela*, Guayana local

GUERCHE(S) - (monetary unit) - *Ethiopia* or *Saudi Arabia*

GUERNSEY - *Great Britain*, Channel Islands

GUGH ISLAND - Great Britain, private local issue

GUINE (PORTUGUESA or **PORTUGUEZA)** - alone or as overprint on stamps of Cape Verde - *Portuguese Guinea*

GUINE BISSAU - *Guinea - Bissau*

GUINEA (CONTI^{AL}) (ESPAÑOLA) - alone or as overprint on stamps of Spain - *Spanish Guinea*

GUINEA CONTINENTAL - overprint on stamps of Elobey, Annobon and Corisco - *Spanish Guinea*

GUINEA ECUATORIAL - *Equatorial Guinea*

GUINEA ESPANOLA - *Spanish Guinea*

GUINEE (FRANÇAISE) - *French Guinea*
- also *Republic of Guinea*

GÜLTIG 9. ARMEE - overprint on stamps of Germany or Romania postal tax - *Romania*, German occupation

GUTEGR. - (monetary unit) - *German States*, Brunswick

GUYANA INDEPENDENCE 1966 - overprint on stamps of British Guiana - *Guyana*

GUY. FRANÇ., **GUYANE** or **GUYANE FRANÇAISE** - alone or as overprint on stamps of France or French Colonies - *French Guiana*

G.W. - overprint on stamps of Cape of Good Hope - *Griqualand West*

GWALIOR - *India*, Gwalior State

- H -

HA - overprint on stamps of Russia - *Siberia*

HAMBURG - *German States*, Hamburg

HAMBURG AMERICAN PACKET COMPANY - Hamburg American Line (Hapag) private issue

HAMMERFEST BYPOST - *Norway* local

HANKOW L.P.O. - *China*, local post

HANNOVER - *German States*, Hanover

HARPER - on registry stamp with no country name - *Liberia*

HASHEMITE - *Jordan*, Transjordan

HATAY DEVLETI - alone or as overprint on stamps of Turkey - *Hatay*

HAUTE SILESIE - *Upper Silesia*

HAUTE VOLTA - alone or as overprint on stamps of Upper Senegal and Niger - *Burkina Faso* (former Upper Volta)

HAUT SENEGAL-NIGER - *Upper Senegal and Niger*

HBA - overprint on stamps of Russia - *Siberia*

H.E.H. THE NIZAM'S - *India*, Hyderabad State

HEJAZ & NEJD or **HEDJAZ & NEDJDE** - *Saudi Arabia*, Kingdom of Hejaz-Nejd

HELLAS* - *Greece*

HELLER - (monetary unit) - Austria, Bosnia and Herzegovina, Carinthia, German East Africa or Liechtenstein

HELSINGFORS - *Norway* local post

HELVETIA* - *Switzerland*

HERM ISLAND - Great Britain - Guernsey local carriage label

HERZOGTH(UM) HOLSTEIN - *German States*, Schleswig - Holstein

HERZOGTH. SCHLESWIG - *German States*, Schleswig - Holstein

H.H.NAWAB SHAH JAHANBECAM (or **N**) - *India*, Bhopal State

H.I. (& U.S.) POSTAGE - *United States*, Hawaii

HILBRE - Great Britain, publicity label

HIMRIYYA - Sharjah, bogus

HIRLAPJEGY or **HIRLAP BELYEC** - *Hungary*, newspaper or newspaper tax

HOHE-RINNE - Hungary, hotel post

HOI HAO - overprint on stamps of Indochina - *France*, Offices in China

HOLKAR STATE - *India*, Indore State

HOLMESTRAND BYPOST - Norway, local post

HOLTE LAND POST - Denmark, local post

HONDA - overprint on stamps of Colombia - *Colombia*, Tolima State

HORSENS BYPOST - Denmark, local post

H.P. - followed by Cyrillic letters - *Bulgaria*

HRVATSKA (SHS) - alone or as overprint on stamps of Hungary - *Yugoslavia*, issues for Croatia-Slavonia

HRVATSKA (with **N.D.** or **NEZAVISNA DRZAVA**) - alone or as overprint on stamps of Yugoslavia - *Yugoslavia*, Croatia (with **REPUBLIKA**) - *Croatia*

HRZGL. POST F.R.M. (or **FRMRK**) - *German states*, Schleswig - Holstein

HT. SENEGAL - **NIGER** - *Upper Senegal & Niger*

HUTT RIVER PROVINCE - Australia, local stamps of secessionist state

HYDERABAD - *India*, Hyderabad feudatory state

- I -

I.B. - On stamps inscribed "Republik Indonesia" - *West Irian*

ICHANG - China, local

I.E.F. "D" - overprint on Turkish revenue stamps - *Mesopotamia* Mosul issue

IERUSALEM - overprint on stamps of Russia - *Russia*, Offices in Turkey

IKAPIAE - *Greece*, Aegean Islands - Icaria

ILE de la Réunion - *Reunion*

ILE ROUAD - overprint on stamps of French Offices in the Levant - *Rouad*

ILES WALLIS ET (or **&**) **FUTUNA** - alone or as overprint on stamps of New Caledonia - *Wallis and Futuna Islands*

IMPER. REG. POSTA AUSTR. - *Austria*, Offices in Turkey

IMPERIAL BRITISH EAST AFRICA COMPANY - *British East Africa*

IMPERIO COLONIAL PORTUGUES - with no colony name - *Portuguese Africa*, postage due

IMPTO (or **IMPUESTO**) **DE GUERRA** - *Puerto Rico* or *Spain*, war tax

IMPUESTO PATRIOTICO - Spain, non-postage

IN CI YIL DONUMU - preceded by "75" - *Turkey*, postal tax

INDE FRANÇAISE (or **FCAISE**) or **INDIE** - *French India*

INDEPENDENCE 11th November 1965 - overprint on stamps of

Southern Rhodesia - *Rhodesia* (formerly Southern Rhodesia)

INDIA - With inscriptions in Portuguese or the words Port., Portugueza, Reis, Real, Republica Portuguesa, Tangas or Rupia - *Portuguese India*

INDO CHINE - alone or as overprint on stamps of France - *Indochina*

INDONESIA - preceded by "N.R." - Indonesia, Sumatra local
- preceded by "Republik" - *Indonesia*
- alone or as overprint on stamps of Netherlands Indies - *Netherlands Indies*

INDORE - *India*, Indore State

INHAMBANE - alone or as overprint on stamps of Mozambique - *Inhambane*

INKERI or **I.N.K.E.R.I.** - *North Ingermanland*

INLAND 3 CENTS - *Liberia*

INRIKES POST - *Sweden*, discount postage

INSELPOST - overprint on stamps of Germany - *Germany*, airmail to German troops in Crete, the Greek Islands and Rhodes

INSTRUÇAO D.L.nº.7 de 32-1934 - overprint on stamps of Portuguese India - *Timor*

INSTRUCCION - *Venezuela*, revenue stamps - some authorized for postage

INSUFFICIENTLY PREPAID, POSTAGE DUE - *Zanzibar*

IONIKON KPATOΣ - *Ionian Islands*, British

I.O.V.R. - *Romania*, postal tax

IQUIQUE - on Peru - *Peru*, canceled in Chile

IRANIENNES - *Iran*

IRAQ IN BRITISH OCCUPATION - overprint on stamps of Turkey - *Mesopotamia*

IRIAN BARAT - on stamp inscribed "Republik Indonesia" or as overprint on stamps of Indonesia - *West Irian* (West New Guinea)

I.R.IRAN - *Iran*

ISLA DE CUBA - *Cuba*, Spanish administration

ISLA DE PASCUA - *Chile*, Easter Island

ISLAMIC REPUBLIC OF IRAN - *Iran*

ISLAND - *Iceland*

ISLAS GALAPAGOS - *Ecuador*, Galapagos Islands

ISO - Sweden, bogus local post

ISOLE ITALIANE DELL'EGEO - overprint on stamps of Italy - *Italy*, Aegean Islands

ISOLE JONIE - overprint on stamps of Italy - *Ionian Islands*, Italian occupation

ISTRA SLOVENSKO PRIMORJE or **ISTRIA LITTORALE SLOVENSKO** - *Yugoslavia*, Istria and the Slovene Coast

ITA-KARJALA - on semipostal stamp inscribed "Suomi - Finland" or as overprint on stamps of Finland - *Karelia*, Finnish occupation

ITALIA* or **ITALIANE** - *Italy*

ITALIA OCCUPAZIONE MILITARE ITALIANA ISOLE CEFALONIA e ITACA - overprint on stamps of pairs of Greece - *Ionian Islands*, Italian occupation

ITALIA REPUBBLICANA FACISTA BASE ATLANTICO - overprint on stamps of Italy - *Italy*, for use in Bordeaux, France 1940-44

ITALII - with "Poczta Polskich" - issued during World War II for use by the Polish Corps and refugees in Italy

IZMIR - **HIMAYEI ETFAL CEMIYETI** - *Turkey*, postal tax

- J -

JAFFA - overprint on stamps of Russia - *Russia*, Offices in Turkey

JAHANBECAM - *India*, Bhopal State

JAIPUR - *India*, Jaipur State

JAMHURI ZANZIBAR (- **TANZANIA**) - *Zanzibar*

JANINA - overprint on stamps of Italy - *Italy*, Offices in Turkey

JAVA - overprint on stamps of Netherlands - *Netherlands Indies*

J.D. (or **JAM. DIM.** or **JUM. DIM.**) **SOOMAALIYA** (or **SOMALIYA** or **SOOMAALIYEED**) - *Somalia*

JEEND, JHIND or **JIND** - overprint on stamps of India - *India*, Jind convention state

JERSEY - *Great Britain*, Channel Islands

JETHOU - Great Britain, Guernsey local issue

JOHOR(E) - alone or as overprint on stamps of Straits Settlements - *Malaya*, Johore or *Malaysia*, Johore

JOURNAUX - *Belgium* or *France*, newspaper stamps

JUBILE DE L'UNION POSTALE UNIVERSELLE - *Switzerland*

JUGOSLAVIJA* - *Yugoslavia*
   - if stamp includes "STT VUJA (or VUJNA)" - *Yugoslavia*, Trieste

- K -

K - (monetary unit - krone) - no country name - *Bosnia & Herzegovina*

K (Numeral) **K** - overprint on stamps of Russia - *Armenia* or *Far Eastern Republic*

KAISERLICHE KÖNIGLICHE ÖSTERREICHISCHE POST - *Austria*

KAIS. KONIGL. OESTRIC.POST - *Austria*

KAIS.KON(IGE) ZEITUNGS STAMPEL (or **STEMPEL**) - *Austria*, newspaper stamp or *Austria*, Lombardy - Venetia

KALAALLIT NUNAAT or **KALATDLIT NUNAT** - *Greenland*

KALAYAAN NANG PILIPINAS - *Philippines*, Japanese occupation

KAMERUN - alone or as overprint on stamps of Germany - *Cameroun* (see British Cameroons also)

KAMPUCHEA - *Cambodia*

KAP - (monetary unit) - *Latvia*

KAREMA - overprint on stamps of Belgian Congo - not authorized

KARJALA - alone or as overprint on stamps of Finland - *Karelia*

KARKI - overprint on stamps of Italy - *Italy*, Aegean Islands - Calchi

KARLFONDS - with "K und K Feldpost" - *Austria*
   - with "K und K Militarpost" - *Bosnia and Herzegovina*

Kärnten Abftimmung - overprint on stamps of Austria - *Austria*, semipostal for Carinthia Plebiscite

KAROLINEN - alone or as overprint on stamps of Germany - *Caroline Islands*

KASAI or **SOUTH KASAI** - Congo, unrecognized state

KATANGA - alone or as overprint on stamps of Congo - secessionist province of Congo -
not recognized

KATHIRI STATE OF SEIYUN - with "Aden" - *Aden*, Kathiri State of Seiyun
- with South Arabia overprint - not recognized

KAULBACH ISLANDS - Canada, local carrier service

K.C.NOVITA - *Serbia*

KEDAH - *Malaya* or *Malaysia*, Kedah State

KEELING ISLANDS - *Cocos Islands*

KELANTAN - *Malaya*, or *Malaysia*, Kelantan State

KENETA - (monetary unit) - *United States*, Hawaii

KENTTAPOSTI(A) - *Finland*, military stamp

KENYA AND UGANDA - *Kenya, Uganda and Tanzania*

KERMADECS - local stamp, Pacific island

KERS - Canada, bogus local

KEWKIANG - China, Treaty Port local

K.G.C.A. - overprint on stamps of Yugoslavia - *Yugoslavia*, semipostal for Carinthia plebiscite

KGL.BAYER.STADTEISENB. - Bavaria railway stamps

KGL.POST FRIMÆRKE (or **FR.M.**) - *Danish West Indies* (if monetary unit is cents)
- *Denmark* (if monetary unit is skillings)

KHMERE - *Cambodia*

KHOR FAKKAN - Sharjah Dependency (not listed by Scott)

KIAUTSCHOU - *Kiauchau*

KIBRIS (CUMHURIYETI) - *Cyprus*

KIBRIS TURK FEDERE DEVLETI (POSTALARI) or **KIBRIS TURK YONETIMI** - Turkish Republic of Northern Cyprus

KIGOMA - overprint on stamps of Belgian Congo - not authorized

KINDERSTEMPEL - play stamp

KINGDOM OF YEMEN - *Yemen*

KIONGA - overprint on stamps of Lourenço Marques - *Kionga*

KISHENGARH - *India*, Kishangarh Feudatory State

K.K.ÖSTERREICHISCHE POST - *Austria*

K.K.POST (ZEITUNGS) STAMPEL (or **STEMPEL**) - *Austria*, or *Austria*, Lombardy-Venetia

KLAIPÉDA - *Memel*, Lithuanian occupation

KOH or **KON** - (monetary unit) - Batum, Far Eastern Republic, Finland, Latvia, Russia, South Russia or White Russia

KOLDING BYPOST - *Denmark*, local post

KONINKRUK DER NEDERLANDEN - *Netherlands*

KONGELIGT POST - *Denmark*

KOP. - (monetary unit) - *Finland*

KORCA or **KORCE(S)** - *Albania*

KORONA - (monetary unit) - *Hungary* or *Poland*

KORUNA - (monetary unit) - *Czechoslovakia*

KOUANG TCHEOU (WAN) - overprint on stamps of Indochina - *France*, Offices in China - Kwangchowan

KOWEIT - overprint on stamps of India - *Kuwait*

KPHTH* - *Crete*

KRAGEROE - *Norway*, local post

KRALJEVSTVO SHS - overprint on stamps of Bosnia and Herzegovina - *Yugoslavia*, issues for Bosnia and Herzegovina

KRALJEVSTVO (or KRALJEVINA) SRBA, HRVATA I SLOVENACA - alone or as overprint on stamps of Bosnia and Herzegovina - *Yugoslavia*

KR. or **KREUZER** - (monetary unit) - Austria, Germany, German States, or Hungary

KRISTIANSUNDS BYPOST - *Norway*, local

KRONA - (monetary unit) - *Iceland* or *Sweden*

KRONE(N) - (monetary unit) - Austria, Bosnia and Herzegovina, Denmark, Fiume, or Western Ukraine

KROON(I) - (monetary unit) - *Estonia*

KRUNA - (monetary unit) - *Montenegro*

K.S.A. - *Saudi Arabia*

K.U.K.MILIT.VERWALTUNG MONTENEGRO - overprint on stamps of Austria - *Montenegro*, Austrian occupation

KUME SHIMA - *Ryukyu Islands*, provisional issue

K. UND (or U.) K. FELDPOST - alone or as overprint on stamps of Bosnia and Herzegovina - *Austria*, military stamp
- with monetary unit bani or lei - *Romania*, Austrian occupation
- surcharged in centesimi or lire - *Italy*, Austrian occupation

K. UND (or U.) K. MILITARPOST - *Bosnia and Herzegovina*

KURHAUS AUF DEN HOHEN RINNE - Hungary, hotel post

KURLAND - overprint on stamps of Germany - *Latvia*, German occupation of Kurzeme

KURORT STOOS - Switzerland hotel post

KURUS(H) - (monetary unit) - *Hatay* or *Turkey*

KUSTENDJE & CZERNAWODA - Romania local

KUWAIT - alone or as overprint on stamps of India or Great Britain - *Kuwait*

KUZEY KIBRIS TURK CUMHURIYETI - *Turkish Republic of Northern Cyprus*

K.WURTT. (POST) - *German States*, Wurttemberg

KYAT - (monetary unit) - *Burma*

KYRGYZSTAN - formerly Kirigizia, U.S.S.R.

- L -

LA AGUERA - overprint on stamps of Rio de Oro or with "Sahara Occidental" - *Aguera (La)*

LABRADOR USA POSTAGE - bogus

LABUAN - overprint on stamps of North Borneo - *Labuan*

L.A.C. - Colombia tuberculosis label

LA CANEA - overprint on stamps of Italy - *Italy*, Offices in Crete

LA CRUZ ROJA ESPAÑOLA - *Spain*, semipostal

LA GEORGIE - *Georgia*

LA GUAIRA - *Venezuela*, La Guaira local

LAIBACH - alone or as overprint on stamps of Italy - *Yugoslavia*, German occupation of Ljubljana (Laibach)

LAJTA BANSAG - Western Hungary, unrecognized

LANDESPOST BERLIN - *Germany*, Berlin

LAND - **POST PORTO MARKE** - *German States*, Baden rural postage due

LANDSTORMEN - overprint on stamps of Sweden - *Sweden* semipostal

LANSA - *Colombia* airmail

LAO - *Laos*

L.A.R. - *Libya*

LAS BELA - *India*, Las Bela feudatory state

LATTAQUIE - overprint on stamps of Syria - *Latakia*

LATVIJA, LATVIJAS PSR or **LATWIJA(S)** - alone or as overprint on stamps of Russia - *Latvia*

LEGIPOSTA - *Hungary* airmail

LEI or **LEU** - (monetary unit) - *Romania*
      - overprint on stamps of Austria - *Romania*, Austrian occupation

LEK - (monetary unit) - *Albania*

LEPTA - (monetary unit) - Corfu, Crete, Epirus or Greece

LERO(S) - overprint on stamps of Italy - *Italy*, Aegean Islands - Lero

LESOTHO - overprint on stamps of Basutoland - *Lesotho*

L'ETAT DE KATANGA - Congo, unrecognized state

LEV(A) - (monetary unit) - *Bulgaria*

LEVANGER BYPOST - Norway local post

LEVANT - with "Poste Française" - *France*, Offices in Turkey
      - overprint on stamps of Poland - *Poland*, Offices in Turkey
      - overprint on stamps of Great Britain - *Great Britain*, Offices in Turkey

LEVANTE - overprint on stamps of Italy - *Italy*, Offices in Turkey

LIBAN or **LIBANAISE** - *Lebanon*

LIBAU - overprint on stamps of Germany - *Latvia*, German occupation

LIBIA, LIBYA or **LIBYE** - alone or as overprint on stamps of Italy, Cyrenaica or Tripolitania - *Libya*

LIBRA - (weight unit) - *Spain*, official

LIETUVA or **LIETUVOS** - alone or as overprint on stamps of Russia - *Lithuania*

LIGNES AERIENNES F.A.F.L. or **LIGNES AERIENNES DE LA FRANCE LIBRE** - *Syria*, Free French Administration

LIHOU - Great Britain, private local issue

LIMA - *Peru*
      - overprint on stamps of Chile - *Peru*, Chilean occupation

LIMBAGAN 1593-1943 - overprint on stamps of Philippines - *Philippines*, Japanese occupation

LINIA AUTORAHTI BUSSFRAKT - *Finland* parcel post

LIPSO - overprint on stamps of Italy - *Italy*, Aegean Islands - Lisso

LIRE - (monetary unit) - alone or as overprint on stamps of Austria - *Italy*

LIRE DI CORONA - (monetary unit) - overprint on Italy special delivery - *Dalmatia*

LISBOA - *Portugal*, postal tax

LISSO - overprint on stamps of Italy - *Italy*, Aegean Islands - Lisso

LITAS - (monetary unit) - *Lithuania*

LITWA SRODKOWA or **LITWY SRODKOWEJ** - *Central Lithuania*

LJUBLJANSKA - overprint on stamps of Italy - *Yugoslavia*, German occupation of Ljubljana (Laibach)

LKT - With "C," "C" & "P" - local issue for British port of Wei-Hai - Wei, China

L.L.L.R. - *Georgia*

L. (or **LOURENÇO**) **MARQUES** - alone or as overprint on stamps of Mozambique - *Lourenco Marques* (Some surcharged Lourenco Marques stamps, with or without "Porteado," are Mozambique.)

L.Mᶜ.L. - As monogram with ship - *Trinidad*, ship stamp

LOJA FRANCA - *Ecuador*, control overprint

LOKALBREF - *Sweden* city postage

L.O.P.P. - *Poland* , semiofficial airmail

LOSEN - *Sweden*, postage due

LOTHRINGEN - overprint on stamps of Germany - *France*, German occupation of Lorraine

L.P. - overprint with double-barred cross on Russia - *Latvia*, Russian occupation

LTSR - overprint on stamps of Lithuania - *Lithuania*, Russian occupation

LUBECK or **LUEBECK** - *German States*, Lubeck

LUBIANA - overprint on stamps of Yugoslavia - *Yugoslavia*, Italian occupation of Ljubljana

LUFTFELDPOST - *Germany*, military airmail

LUNDY ISLANDS - Great Britain, private local issue

LUXEMBURG - overprint on stamps of Germany - *Luxembourg*, German occupation

- **M** -

MACAU or **MACAV** - *Macao*

MADAGASCAR - overprint on stamps of France or French Colonies - *Madagascar*

MADEIRA - overprint on stamps of Portugal - *Madeira* (see under Portugal also)

MADERANERTHAL - Switzerland, hotel post

MADRID - *Spain*

MAFEKING BESIEGED - overprint on stamps of Bechuanaland Protectorate or Cape of Good Hope - *Cape of Good Hope*

MAFEKING SIEGE - *Cape of Good Hope*

MAFIA - overprint on stamps of German East Africa or India - *German East Africa*, British occupation of Mafia (not listed by Scott)

MAGDALENA - *Colombia*, Department of Magdalena

MAGYAR (KIR POSTA), MAGYARORSZAG or **MAGYAR TANACSKOZTARSASAG** - *Hungary*

MAGY. KIR. HIRLAP BELYEG, - *Hungary*

MAHDI - with "Postes Soudan" - bogus

MAHRA STATE - *Aden* (not listed by Scott)

MAHRA SULTANATE OF QISHN AND SOCOTRA - *South Arabia* locals

M.A.L. - (monetary unit) - surcharge on Great Britain - *Great Britain,* Offices in Tripolitania

MALACCA - *Malaya* or *Malaysia,* Malacca State

MALAGA LIBERADA - overprint on stamps of Spain, *Spain,* Malaga issue

MALAGASY - *Madagascar*

MALAYA SINGAPORE - *Singapore*

MALAYA STRAITS SETTLEMENTS - *Straits Settlements*

MALAYAN POSTAL UNION - *Malaya,* postage due

MALAYSIA SARAWAK - *Sarawak*

MALDIVES - alone or as overprint on stamps of Ceylon - *Maldive Islands*

MALGACHE - *Madagascar*

MALMEDY - overprint on stamps of Belgium - *Germany,* Belgian occupation

MALMO GAMLA - *Sweden,* locals

MALUKU SELETAN - South Moluccas, bogus

MANAMA - Ajman locals, not recognized

MANDAL BYPOST - Norway locals

MAN, ISLE OF - *Great Britain,* Channel Islands

MANDATED TERRITORY OF TANGANYIKA - *Tanganyika*

MANIZALES - *Colombia,* Antioquia local

MANUEL E. JIMENEZ - *Colombia,* Cauca Department, receipt label

MAPKA - Azerbaijan, Finland, Russia or Serbia

MARCA DA BOLLO - *Italy*

MARIANAS ESPAÑOLAS - overprint on stamps of Philippines - *Mariana Islands*

MARIANEN - alone or as overprint on stamps of Germany - *Mariana Islands*

MARIENWERDER - overprint on stamps of Germany - *Marienwerder*

MARK - (monetary unit) - *Estonia, Finland* or *Germany*

MARKA - (monetary unit) - *Estonia* or *Poland*

MARKKA(A) - (monetary unit) - *Finland*

MAROC - *French Morocco* or *Morocco*
    - with "Royaume de" - *Morocco*

MAROCCO or **MAROKKO** - overprint on stamps of Germany - *Germany,* Offices in Morocco

MAROTIRI ISLAND - New Zealand local

MARRUECOS - alone or as overprint on stamps of Spain - *Spanish Morocco,* or *Morocco,* Northern Zone

MARSCHALL (or **MARSHALL**) **INSELN** - alone or as overprint on stamps of Germany - *Marshall Islands*

MARSHALL ISLANDS - *United States,* Trust Territory - Republic of the Marshall Islands

MARTINIQUE - alone or as overprint on stamps of French Colonies - *Martinique*

MATABELELAND - *Rhodesia* local

MATURIN - *Venezuela,* Maturin State locals

MAURITANIE - *Mauritania*
    - with surcharge - *Mauritania* or *French West Africa*

MAYREAU ISLAND - *St. Vincent Grenadines*

MAZAGAN - **(AZENOUR)** - **MARAKECH** - Morocco local

M.B.D. - overprint on stamps of India - *India*, Nandgaon State

MBLEDHJA (or **E**) **KUSHTETUESE** - overprint on stamps of Albania - *Albania*, Italian Dominion

MBRETNIA SHQYPTARE - *Albania*

MBRETNIJA SHQIPTARE - *Albania*, Italian Dominion

MECKLENB. SCHWERIN - *German States*, Mecklenburg - Schwerin

MECKLENB. STRELITZ - *German States*, Mecklenburg - Strelitz

MECKLENBURG VORPOMMERN (or **MECKLBG** - **VORPOMM**) - *Germany*, Soviet Zone - Mecklenburg - Western Pomerania

MEDELLIN - *Colombia*, Antioquia Department provisionals or private issues

MEDIO REAL - (monetary unit) - *Dominican Republic*

M.E.F. - overprint on stamps of Great Britain - *Great Britain*, Offices in Africa

MEJICO - *Mexico*

MELAYU - *Malaya*

MEMEL or **MEMELGEBIET** - overprint on stamps of France or Germany - *Memel*
- with "Klaipeda" - *Memel*, Lithuanian occupation

MELILLA - Morocco military label

MENGE - (monetary unit) - *Mongolia*

METALIK - *Crete*, Russian sphere, District of Rethymnon

METELIN - overprint on stamps of Russia - *Russia*, Offices in Turkey

MEXICANO - *Mexico*

MIASTA PRZEDBORZA - Poland local

MICRONESIA - *United States*, Trust Territory - Federated States of Micronesia

MILITARPOST EILMARKE (or **PORTOMARKE**) - *Bosnia and Herzegovina*
- surcharged in centesimi - *Italy*, Austrian occupation

MILL. or **MILLIEMES** - (monetary unit) - surcharge on stamps of France - *France*, Offices in Egypt

M. KIR - *Hungary*

M. KIR. POSTATAKARER PENZTAR - *Hungary*, postal savings stamp, (one valid for postage)

MN - (monetary unit) - *Korea*

MOÇAMBIQUE - *Mozambique*

MODONES(I) - *Italian States*, Modena

MOGADOR MARRAKESCH - Morocco local post

MOLDOVA - former U.S.S.R. Republic of Moldova

MON - (monetary unit) - *Japan*

MONASTIR - overprint on stamps of Turkey - *Turkey*

MONGTSEU, **MONG-TSEU** or **MONGTZE** - surcharge on stamps of Indochina - *France*, Offices in China

MONROVIA - On registry stamp - *Liberia*

MONT ATHO(S) - overprint on stamps of Russia - *Russia*, Offices in Turkey

MONTENEGRO - overprint on stamps of Austria - *Montenegro*, Austrian occupation

30

- overprint on stamps of Yugoslavia - *Montenegro*, German or Italian occupation

MONTERREY - *Mexico*, Monterrey provisional issue, considered bogus

MONTEVIDEO - *Uruguay*

MONTSERRAT - alone or as overprint on stamps of Antigua - *Montserrat*

MOQUEA or **MOQUEGUA** - overprint on stamps of Peru or Arequipa Province of Peru - *Peru*, Moquegua Province

MORELIA - *Mexico*, Morelia provisional issue, considered bogus

MOROCCO AGENCIES - overprint on stamps of Gibraltar or Great Britain - *Great Britain*, Offices in Morocco

MORVI - *India*, Morvi feudatory state

MOSTRA - *Italy*, specimen

MOYEN CONGO* - *Middle Congo*

MQE - overprint on stamps of French Colonies - *Martinique*

MUESTRA - Spanish for "Specimen"

MULTA - Chile, Costa Rica, Ecuador or Portugal - postage due

MUNG - (monetary unit) - *Mongolia*

MUSCAT AND OMAN - *Oman*

MUSTER - German for "Specimen"

MUSTIQUE ISLAND - *St. Vincent Grenadines*

MUTAWAKELITE (or **MOUTAWAKILITE**) **KINGDOM OF YEMEN** - *Yemen*

MUUNGANO - *Zanzibar*

M.V.i.R. - overprint on stamps of Germany or Russia - *Romania*, German occupation

MYANMAR - new name for *Burma*

- **N** -

NABHA STATE - overprint on stamps of India - *India*, Nabha Convention State

NACIONES UNIDAS - *United Nations*

NAGALAND - India, propaganda labels

NAMSOS BYPOST - Norway locals

NANDGAM - *India*, Nandgaon feudatory state

NANKING - *China* Treaty Port local

NAPA or **NAPE** - (monetary unit) - *Montenegro* or *Serbia*

NAPOLETANA - *Italian States*, Two Sicilies

NA SLASK - surcharge - *Central Lithuania*, semipostal

NATIONALER VERWALTUNGSAUSSCHUSS - overprint on stamps of Montenegro - *Montenegro*, German occupation

NATIONS UNIES - *United Nations*, Offices in Geneva

NAURU - alone or as overprint on stamps of Great Britain - *Nauru*

NAWABSHAH JAHANBECAM - *India*, Bhopal State

NAYE PAISE - (monetary unit) - *India* and most Arab sheikhdoms

N.C.E. - overprint on stamps of French Colonies - *New Caledonia*

N.D.HRVATSKA - *Croatia*

NEDERLAND* - *Netherlands*

NED(ERLANDSCH) (or **NEDERL.**) **INDIE** - *Netherlands Indies*

NED(ERLANDSE) ANTILLEN - *Netherlands Antilles*

NED(ERLANDS) NIEUW GUINEA - *Netherlands New Guinea*

NEGRI SEMBILAN - alone or as overprint on stamps of Straits Settlements *Malaya*, Negri Sembilan

NEGERI SEMBILAN - *Malaysia*, Negri Sembilan

NE PAS LIVRER LE DIMANCHE - *Belgium* ("Do not deliver on Sunday" tab)

NEW GUINEA - with "British" - *Papua New Guinea*
- with "Territory" - *New Guinea*

NEW HEBRIDES (CONDOMINIUM) - alone or as overprint on stamps of Fiji - *New Hebrides*, British issue

NEZ(AVISNA) DRZ(AVA) HRVATSKA - *Croatia*

N.F. - overprint on stamps of Nyasaland Protectorate - *German East Africa*, British occupation

N.fl. - *Armenia*

NIEUW GUINEA - *Netherlands New Guinea*

NIEUWE REPUBLIEK - *New Republic*

NIPPON - *Japan* (A three-character overprint may indicate stamp is a "mihon" or specimen.)

NISIRO(S) - overprint on stamps of Italy - *Italy*, Aegean Islands - Nisiro

NIUAFO'OU - *Tonga* (Tin Can Island) - not listed by Scott

NIUE - alone or as overprint on stamps of New Zealand - *Niue*

NLLE CALEDONIE - alone or as overprint on stamps of French Colonies - *New Caledonia*

N.M.S. - Madagascar - locals of Norwegian Missionary Society

NO HAY ESTAMPILLAS - "There are no stamps" - *Colombia*, receipt labels

NORD-DEUTSCHE-POST or **NORDDEUTSCHER POST BEZIRK** - *German States*, North German Confederation

NOREG or **NORGE** - *Norway*

NORFOLK ISLAND - alone or as overprint on stamps of Australia - *Norfolk Island*

NOSSI-BÉ - overprint on stamps of French Colonies - *Nossi Bé*

NOUVELLE (or **NOULLE.**) **CALÉDONIE** - *New Caledonia*

NOUVELLES HEBRIDES - alone or as overprint on stamps of New Caledonia - *New Hebrides* - French issue
- with "Syndicat Français" - New Hebrides local

NOWANUGGUR - *India*, Nowanuggur feudatory state

NOWTA - *Serbia* or *Ukraine*

NOWTE - *Montenegro*

N.P. - (monetary unit) - surcharge on stamps of Great Britain - *Oman*

N.R.INDONESIA - Indonesia, Sumatra local

N S B - overprint on stamps of French Colonies - *Nossi Bé*

N.SEMBILAN - *Malaya*, Negri Sembilan

N.S.W. - *New South Wales*

NUEVA GRANADA - *Colombia*

N.W.PACIFIC ISLANDS - overprint on stamps of Australia - *North West Pacific Islands*

NYASSA - alone or as overprint on stamps of Mozambique - *Nyassa* (Portuguese)

NYUGAT - MAGYARORSZAG ORSZVE - overprint on stamps of Hun-

gary - Western Hungary (not listed by Scott)
N.Z. - *New Zealand*

- O -

OAHAMAPKA - *Finland*
OAXACA - *Mexico*, civil war issue
OBOCK - overprint on stamps of French Colonies - *Obock*
 - surcharged - *Somali Coast*
OCCUPATION AZIRBAYEDJAN - overprint on stamps of Russia - Azerbaijan, private overprint
OCCUPATION FRANÇAISE - overprint on stamps of Hungary - *Hungary*, French occupation
OCCUSSI-AMBENO - Timor, phantom issue
OCEANIE - *French Polynesia*
ODENSE BYPOST - *Denmark* local
ŒSTERREICH - alone or as overprint on stamps of Germany - *Austria*
ŒSTERR. POST - *Austria*
 - with "Liechtenstein" - *Liechtenstein*, Austrian postal administration
OEUVRES DE SOLIDARITE FRANÇAISE - *French Colonies*, semipostal
O.F.CASTELLORISO - overprint on stamps of France - *Castellorizo*
OFF(ENTLIG) SAK - *Norway*, Officials
OFFICIAL - overprint on stamps inscribed "Kenya Uganda Tanganyika"- *Tanganyika*
OFFICIAL (or **OFFISIEEL**)(**S.W.A.**) - overprint on stamps of South Africa - *South West Africa*
OHU POST - *Estonia* airmail
OIL RIVERS - overprint on stamps of Great Britain - *Niger Coast Protectorate*
OKCA - *Russia*, Army of the North
OLDENBURG - *German States*, Oldenburg
OLSZTYN-ALLENSTEIN - overprint on stamps of Germany - *Allenstein*
OLTRE GUIBA - overprint on stamps of Italy - *Oltre Guiba*
OMAN IMAMATE STATE - not valid issues
OMAN, STATE OF - phantom issues ("Sultanate of Oman" is valid)
O.M.F. CILICIE - overprint on stamps of France - *Cilicia*
O.M.F. SYRIE - overprint on stamps of French Offices in Turkey - *Syria*
ONE ANNA - on stamp with sun face in circle - *India*, Jasdan native state
O.N.F.CASTELLORIZO - overprint on stamps of French Offices in Turkey - *Castellorizo*
ONZA - (weight unit) - *Spain*, Official
OPLATA SKARBOWA - *Poland*, revenue stamp
ORANGE RIVER COLONY - overprint on stamps of Cape of Good Hope - *Orange River Colony*
ORANJE VRIJ STAAT* - *Orange River Colony* (Orange Free State)
ORCHA or **ORCHHA** - *India*, Orchha feudatory state
ORE - (monetary unit) - Denmark, Greenland, Norway and Sweden
ORTS-POST - *Switzerland*, federal administration
ORVAL - *Belgium*

O.S. - with no country name - *Norway*, Officials

O.S. G.R.I. - overprint on stamps of German New Guinea - *New Britain*, Official

OSMANLI POSTALARI 1337 - overprint on Turkish revenue stamps - *Turkey in Asia*

OSTEN - overprint on stamps of Germany - *Poland*, German occupation

ÖSTERREICH - alone or as overprint on stamps of Germany - *Austria*

ÖSTERREICHISCHE (or **ÖSTERR.**) **POST** - *Austria*

OSTLAND - overprint on stamps of Germany - *Russia*, German occupation

OTVORENIE SLOVENSKEHO - *Czechoslovakia* surcharge

OUBANGUI-CHARI (-TCHAD) - alone or as overprint on stamps of France or Middle Congo - *Ubangi - Shari*

OXIA - bogus issue

OZ. - on stamp with ship and "P," "S," "N" and "C" in corners - *Peru*

- P -

P. - with star and crescent in oval - overprint on stamps of Straits Settlements - *Malaya*, Perak
- surcharge on stamps of Turkey, with Arabic writing followed by "1" - *Thrace*
- with queen's cameo but no country name - *Great Britain*

P (numeral) **P** - *Switzerland*, franchise stamp

PABAY - Great Britain, publicity label before 1972; private local issue thereafter

PACCHI POSTALI - with "SUL BOLLETTINO - SULLA RICEVUTA" - *Italy* parcel post
- with "BOLLETTA RICEVUTA" - *San Marino* parcel post
- with star and crescent emblem or Arabic writing - *Somalia* parcel post

PACKENMARKA - *Russia* - Wenden

PACKHOI or **PAKHOI** - overprint on stamps of Indochina - *France*, Offices in China

PAHANG - *Malaya* or *Malaysia*, Pahang

PAISA - (monetary unit) - Afghanistan, Bangladesh, India, Nepal or Pakistan

PAITA - overprint on stamps of Peru - *Peru*, Paita provisional issue

PAKISTAN - alone or as overprint on stamps of India - *Pakistan*

PAKKE-PORTO - *Greenland*, parcel post

PALESTINE - overprint on stamps inscribed "EEF" with Hebrew or Arabic characters - *Palestine*, British occupation
- overprint on stamps of Egypt - *Egypt*, Palestine occupation

PAPUA - alone or as overprint on stamps of British New Guinea - *Papua New Guinea*

PALAU - *United States*, trust territory - Republic of Palau

PAQUETE - *Chile* or *Venezuela*

PARA(S) - (monetary unit) - Egypt, Turkey or Yugoslavia
- overprint on stamps of Austria, France, Germany, Great Britain, Italy, Romania or Russia - Offices in Turkey of the respective

countries

PARIS 1931 - with no colony name - *France*

PARM, PARMA or **PARMENSI** - *Italian States*, Parma

PASCO - overprint on stamps of Peru - *Peru*, Pasco provisional

PATIALA (STATE) - *India*, Patiala convention state

PATMO(S) - overprint on stamps of Italy - *Italy*, Aegean Islands - Patmo

PATZCUARO - *Mexico*, Patzcuaro provisional, considered bogus

PCCP or **PCØCP** - *Russia*

PD and numeral - overprint on stamps of French Colonies - *St. Pierre & Miquelon*

PECHINO - overprint on stamps of Italy - *Italy*, Offices in China

PEN, PENNI or **PENNIAS** - (monetary unit) - Estonia, Finland or North Ingermanland

PENANG - *Malaya* or *Malaysia*, Penang

PENRHYN ISLAND - overprint on stamps of Cook Islands or New Zealand - *Penrhyn Island*

PEOPLE'S REPUBLIC OF SOUTHERN YEMEN - alone or as overprint on stamps of South Arabia - *Yemen, People's Democratic Republic*

PERAK - alone or as overprint on stamps of Straits Settlements - *Malaya* or *Malaysia*, Perak

PERLIS - *Malaya* or *Malaysia*, Perlis

PERSANE(S) - *Iran*

PERSE - with "A Perçevoir" - Iran, unissued postage due

PERSEKUTUAN TANAH MELAYU - *Malaya*

PERUANA or **PERV** - *Peru*

PESA - (monetary unit) - overprint on stamps of Germany - *German East Africa*

PESETA(S) - (monetary unit) - with coat of arms showing a llama - *Peru* - otherwise *Spain*

PETIT ST. VINCENT - *St. Vincent Grenadines*

PF. or **PFENNIG(E)** - (monetary unit) - *German States*, Bavaria or Wurttemberg, or *Germany*

PFG - (monetary unit) - surcharge on stamps of Russia - *Estonia*, German occupation

P.G.S. - overprint on stamps of Straits Settlements - *Malaya*, Perak officials

PHILIPPINES - overprint on stamps of the United States - *Philippine Islands*, U.S. dominion

PIASTER - (monetary unit) - overprint on stamps of Austria - *Austria*, Offices in Turkey
- overprint on stamps of Germany - *Germany*, Offices in Turkey

PIASTRA - (monetary unit) - overprint on stamps of Italy - *Italy*, Offices in Crete or Africa

PIASTRE(S) - (monetary unit) - Cyprus, Egypt or Turkey
- overprint on stamps of France, Great Britain, Italy, Romania or Russia - Offices in Turkey of the respective countries

PICE - (monetary unit) - *Nepal*

PIES - (monetary unit) - *India*

PILIPINAS* - *Philippines*

PINSIN(E) - (monetary unit) - *Ireland*

PISAGUA - cancellation on Chile - Chilean occupation of Peru

PISCO - overprint on stamps of Peru - *Peru*, Pisco provisional

PISCOPI - overprint on stamps of Italy - *Italy*, Aegean Islands - Piscopi

PIURA - overprint on stamps of Peru - *Peru*, Piura provisional

PJON(USTU or **USTA)** - *Iceland* Official

PLAN SUR DE VALENCIA - *Spain* obligatory tax stamps

PLATA F. - with Rs. or Rl. - (monetary unit) - *Cuba* or *Philippines*

PLAUEN - *Germany* World War II local

PLEBISCIT SLESVIG - *Schleswig*

PLEBISCITE OLSZTYN ALLENSTEIN - overprint on stamps of Germany - *Allenstein*

POCZTA LITWA SRODKOWA - *Central Lithuania*

POCZTA OSIEDLI POLSKICH ITALII - issued after World War II for the Polish Corps and refugees in Italy

POCZTA POLSKA - alone or as overprint on stamps of Austria or Germany - *Poland*

Poftgebiet Ob. Oft. - see "Postgebiet Ob. Ost"

POHJOIS INKERI - *North Ingermanland*

POLECONA - *Poland*, Officials

POLSKA* - *Poland*

POLSKA POCZTA - overprint on stamps of Austria - *Poland*

POLYNESIE FRANÇAISE - *French Polynesia*

POON - (monetary unit) - *Korea*

POPULAIRE du BENIN - overprint on stamps of Dahomey - *Benin People's Republic*

PORT CANTONAL - *Switzerland*, Cantonal Administration, Geneva

PORTEADO - *Portugal* or Portuguese Colonies, postage due

PORTE DE CONDUCCION - *Peru*, parcel post

PORTE DE MAR - *Mexico*, labels indicating the amount to be paid to sea captains for taking outgoing foreign mail

PORTE FRANCO - *Peru* or *Portugal*

PORT GDANSK - overprint on stamps of Poland - *Poland*, Offices in Danzig

PORT LAGOS - overprint on stamps of France - *France*, Offices in Turkey

PORTO - with no country name - *Austria*
- with "piaster" - *Austria*, Offices in Turkey
- overprint on stamps of Bosnia and Herzegovina - *Yugoslavia*
- as inscription or overprint on stamps of Denmark - *Denmark*, postage due

PORTO GAZETEI - *Romania*, Moldavia

PORTO MÆRKE - *Norway* postage due

PORTO MARKA - *Croatia* postage due

PORTO MARKE - *Bosnia and Herzegovina* postage due

PORTO PFLICHTIGE DIENST SACHE - *German States*, Wurttemberg Official

PORTO RICO - overprint on stamps of the United States - *Puerto Rico*

PORT-SAID - alone or as overprint on stamps of France - *France*, Offices in Egypt

PORTUGUESA or **PORTVGVEZA** - *Portugal* or Portuguese colonies

POSESIONES ESPANOLAS DE AFRICA OCCIDENTAL - with "**HABILITADO PARA CORREOS**" surcharge - *Spanish Guinea*

POSESIONES ESPANOLAS DEL SAHARA OCCIDENTAL - *Spanish Sahara*

POSSEEL-POSTAGE - *South Africa*

POST (NOYTA) - with posthorns in the four corners - *Germany*, Russian issue for East Saxony

POSTA 15 or **35** - overprint on stamps of Tanna Tuva revenue - *Tanna Tuva*

POSTA AUSTR - *Austria*, Offices in Turkey

POSTA with: **AJORE, DI FIUME** (or **FIVME), DI SICILIA, NAPOLETANA, ROMANA, SHQYPINIS** or **TOUVA** - see FIUME, FIVME, SICILIA, NAPOLETANA, ROMANIA, SHQIPENIA and TOUVA

POSTA CESKOSLOVENSKA - overprint on stamps of Austria or Hungary - *Czechoslovakia*

POSTA CESKOSLOVENSKE ARMADY-SIBIRSKE - *Czechoslovakia* Legion Post in Siberia

POSTAGE or **POSTAGE & REVENUE** - *Great Britain* and colonies

POSTAGE - overprint on bisected stamp with queen's head - *Grenada* - with "V" and "R" in corners - *Fiji*

POSTAGE, POST(AGE) & RECEIPT or **POST STAMP** - with values in annas or pies - *India*, Hyderabad

POSTAGE DUE - with values in pence or shillings - *Australia* or *Great Britain* - with values in pinsin - *Ireland*

POSTAGE I.E.F. 'D' - overprint on stamps of Turkey - *Mesopotamia*, Mosul issue

POSTAGES CORREOS 5 CTS. - Puerto Rico (U.S. dominion)

POSTAL UNION CONGRESS LONDON 1929 - *Great Britain*

POSTA MOLDOVA - *Moldova*, former Republic of U.S.S.R.

POSTAS LE NIOC - *Ireland* postage due

POSTAT E QEVER(R)IES SE PERKOHESHME (TE SHQIPENIES) - *Albania*

POSTAT SHQIPTARE - *Albania*

POST COLLI or **POSTCOLLO** - *Belgium* parcel post

POSTE AÉRIENNE or **AERIEO** - with no country name - *Iran* airmail

POSTE with: **COLONIALI ITALIANE, de GENEVE, DI FIUME** (or **FIVME), ESTENSI, ITALIANE, PERSANE** or **VATICANE** - see COLONIALE ITALIANE, GENEVE, FIUME, FIVME, ESTENSI, ITALIANE, PERSANE and VATICANE

POSTE KHEDEVIE EGIZIANE - *Egypt*

POSTE LOCALE - *Switzerland*, Geneva Canton or Federal Administration- Turkey, Liannos's local post

POSTES with: **AFGHANES, EGYPTIENNES, HEDJAZ AND NEDJDE, LAO, OTTOMANES** or **PERSANES** - see AFGHANES, EGYPTIENNES, HEDJAZ AND NEDJDE, LAO, OTTOMANES and PERSANES - with no country name - Belgium, France, French Colonies or Luxembourg - with red crescent and "1954" - *Afghanistan* postal tax

POSTES CENT. (or **CENTIME**) - *Belgium*

- with fine network background - *France*, German occupation of Alsace and Lorraine

POSTES (IMPERIALES) de COREE - *Korea*

POSTES FRANCE (or **PARIS**) **1922** - on France are precancels

POSTES SERBES - overprint on stamps of France - *Serbia* used in Corfu

POSTFAERGE - overprint on stamps of Denmark - *Denmark* parcel post

POSTGEBIET OB. OST. - overprint on stamps of Germany in Germanic type - *Lithuania*, German occupation

POSTMARKE - with crown and "¼ Gutegr." - *German States*, Brunswick

POST SCHILLING - no country name - *German States*, Schleswig-Holstein

POST STAMP - with value in annas or pies - *India*, Hyderabad

POSTZEGEL - *Netherlands* or *Transvaal*

POUL - (monetary unit) - *Afghanistan*

P.P. - overprint in rectangle on French postage due - *French Morocco*

P. (numeral) **P.** - *Switzerland* franchise stamp

PRANGKO TABOENGAU POS - overprint on stamps of Netherlands Indies - Japanese occupation savings stamps

PREUSSEN - *German States*, Prussia

PRINCE FAROUK - *Egypt*

PRINCIPALITY OF THOMOND - bogus label

PRINCIPAUTE de MONACO - *Monaco*

PRINCIPAT D'ANDORRA - *Andorra*

PRISTINA - overprint on stamps of Turkey - *Turkey*

PRIVATPOST - *Sweden*, discount postage

PRO SEMINARIO ZARAGOZA - Spain, non-postal label

PRO (PLEBISCITO) TACNA Y ARICA - *Peru* postal tax

PROTECTORADO ESPAÑOL - alone or as overprint on stamps of Spain - *Spanish Morocco*

PROTECTORADO MARRUECOS - overprint on stamps of Spain - *Spanish Morocco*

PROTECTORATE - overprint on stamps of Bechuanaland - *Bechuanaland Protectorate*

PROTECTORAT FRANÇAIS - overprint on stamps of France or French Morocco - *French Morocco*

PRO TUBERCULOSOS POBRES - *Spain* postal tax

PRO UNION IBEROAMERICANA - *Spain*

PROVINCIA DE CABO VERDE - *Cape Verde*

PROVINCIA DE MACAU - *Macao*

PROVINCIA DE MOÇAMBIQUE - *Mozambique*

PROVINCIE MODONES - *Italian States*, Modena

PROVINZ LAIBACH - overprint on stamps of Italy - *Yugoslavia*, German occupation of Ljubljana (Laibach)

PROVINZ SACHSEN - *Germany*, Russian occupation of Saxony

PROVISIONAL 1881-1882 - overprint on stamps of Peru - *Peru*, Arequipa provisional

PROVISORNI CESKOSLOVENSKA VLADA - overprint on stamps of Austria - private issue

PRUNE ISLAND - *St. Vincent Grenadines*

P.S. - intertwined as a monogram - *Colombia*, Cauca Department

P.S.N.C. - with ship in center and one letter in each corner - *Peru*

P<u>TO</u> (or **PUERTO**) **RICO** - alone or as overprint on stamps of the United States - *Puerto Rico*

PUL - (monetary unit) - *Afghanistan*

PULAU PINANG (or **PENANG**) - *Malaysia*, Penang State

PUNO - *Peru*, Puno provisional

PUOLUSTUSVOIMAT - *Finland*, military stamp

PUTTIALLA - overprint on stamps of India - *India*, Patiala convention state

PYAS - (monetary unit) - *Burma*

- Q -

Q<u>ARKU</u> I KORCES - *Albania*

QATAR - alone or as overprint on stamps of Great Britain - *Qatar*

Q<u>IND</u>(AR) or **Q<u>INT</u>(AR)** - (monetary unit) - *Albania*

QU'AITI STATE IN HADHRAMAUT - with "Aden" - *Aden*
- with South Arabia surcharge - not recognized

QU'AITI STATE OF SHIHR & MUKALLA - with "Aden" - *Aden*

QUAN BUU - *Viet Nam* (South), military stamps

QUELIMANE - overprint on stamps of some Portuguese colonies - *Quelimane*

QUINTA DE GOYA - *Spain*

- R -

R - overprint on stamps of Colombia - *Colombia*, airpost registration, or *Panama*
- black overprint on stamps of Northern Rhodesia - Northern Rhodesia fiscal
- on stamps with inverted heart or fancy design - *India*, Jind feudatory state
- overprint on stamp with Arabic letters, but no country name - *Iran*
- surcharge with value on stamps of France or French Colonies - *Reunion*
- surcharge on stamps of Great Britain - *Oman*

RAJASTHAN - overprint on stamps of India, Jaipur - *India*, Rajasthan feudatory state

RANDERS BYPOST - *Denmark* local

RAPPEN - (monetary unit) - *Liechtenstein* or *Switzerland*

RAROTONGA - alone or as overprint on stamps of New Zealand - *Cook Islands*

RASEINIU - *Lithuania* local

R A U - overprint on stamps of Syria - *Syria*, United Arab Republic

RAYON - *Switzerland*, federal administration

R. COMMISSARIATO CIVILE TERRITORI SLOVENIA OCCUPATI LUBIANA - overprint on stamps of Yugoslavia - *Yugoslavia*, Italian occupation of Ljubljana

R. de C. w. GARZON - *Colombia*, Tolima State (unauthorized)

R. DE PANAMA - overprint on stamps of Colombia - *Panama*

REAL - (monetary unit) - Costa Rica, Cuba, Dominican Republic, Mexico, Puerto Rico or Spain

RECARGO - *Spain* war tax

RECOUVERMENTS - *France* postage due

RECUERDO DEL 1'DE FEBRERO 1916 - *Honduras*

REDONDA - dependency of Antigua (Not listed by Scott)

REGATUL ROMANIEI - overprint on stamps of Hungary - *Hungary*, Romanian occupation

REGENCE DE TUNIS - *Tunisia*

REGNO D'ITALIA - *Italy*

   - overprint on stamps of Austria with "Venezia Giulia" or Trentino" - *Austria*, Italian occupation

   - overprint on stamps inscribed "Fiume" or "Fivme" - *Fiume*

REICH or **REICHSPOST** - *Germany*

REIS - (monetary unit) - with no country name - *Portugal*

REP. (DI) S. MARINO - *San Marino*

REP. ITALIANA - *Italy*

REPOBLIKA MALAGASY - *Madagascar*

REP.O.DEL URUGUAY - *Uruguay*

REPOEBLIK INDONESIA - These and some inscribed "Republik Indonesia" are revolutionary issues, not recognized.

REP. SHQIPTARE - *Albania*

REPUBBLICA DI SAN MARINO - *San Marino*

REPUBBLICA ITALIANA - *Italy*

REPUBBLICA SOCIALE ITALIANA - *Italy*, Italian Socialist Republic

REPUBBLICA SOCIALE ITALIANA BASE ATLANTICA - overprint on stamps of Italy - *Italy*, for use in Bordeaux, France

REPUB. FRANC. - *France* or *French Colonies*

REPUBLICA with: **de GUINEA ECUATORIAL, DOMINICANA, ESPAÑOLA, MOÇAMBIQUE, PERUANA, del PERU, POPULARA ROMINA,** or **PORTUGUESA** - see name following "Republica"

REPUBLICA CONGO - overprint on stamps of various Portuguese colonies - *Portuguese Congo*

REPUBLICA DE LA N'GRANADA - *Colombia*, Cauca Province

REPUBLICA GUINE - overprint on stamps of Macao, Portuguese Africa or Timor - *Portuguese Guinea*

REPUBLICA INHAMBANE - overprint on stamps of Macao, Portuguese Africa or Timor - *Inhambane*

REPUBLICA MAYOR DE CENTRO AMERICA - *Nicaragua*

REPUBLICA ORIENTAL - *Uruguay*

REPUBLICA TETE - alone or as overprint on stamps of Portuguese Colonies - *Tete*

REPUBLIC OF BOTSWANA - overprint on stamps of Bechuanaland Protectorate - *Botswana*

REPUBLIC OF THE MARSHALL ISLANDS - *United States*, trust territory - Marshall Islands

REPUBLICA OF PALAU - *United States*, trust territory - Palau

REPUBLIEK van SUID AFRIKA - *South Africa*

REPUBLIKA HRVATSKA - *Croatia*

REPUBLIKA NG PILIPINAS - *Philippines*

REPUBLIKA POPULLORE (SOCIALISTE) E SHQIPERISE - *Albania*

REPUBLIKA SHQIPTARE - *Albania*

REPUBLIK INDONESIA (SERIKAT) - *Indonesia*

REPUBLIK MALUKU SELATAN - South Moluccas (not recognized)

REPUBLIQUE: ARABE UNIE - *Syria*, issues for United Arab Republic

    AUTONOME DU TOGO - *Togo*

    D'AZERBAIDJAN - *Azerbaijan*

    DEMOCRATIQUE DU CONGO - *Congo Democratic Republic*

    D'HAITI - *Haiti*

    FRANÇAISE - *France* or *French Colonies*. Some with surcharges or overprints are individual French colonies.

    ISLAMIQUE de MAURITANIE - *Mauritania*

    POPULAIRE DU BENIN - alone or as overprint on stamps of Dahomey - *Benin People's Republic*

    POPULAIRE DU KAMPUCHEA - *Cambodia*

    Others - check name following "Republique (De or Du)"

RESMI - *Turkey* Officials

RETYMNO - *Crete*, Russian sphere

RÉUNION - alone or as overprint on stamps of French Colonies - *France*, Reunion

REVENUE AND POSTAGE - Great Britain or colonies or India - Kishengarh

RF - *France* or French colonies

R.F. FEZZAN - overprint on stamps of Italy or Libya - *Libya*, French occupation

R.H. - *Haiti*

RHEINLAND-PFALZ - *Germany*, Rhine Palatinate, French occupation

RHODESIA - overprint on stamps inscribed "British South Africa Company" - *Rhodesia*, (British South Africa)

    - as inscription - *Rhodesia*, formerly Southern Rhodesia

RIAL(S) - (monetary unit) - *Iran*

RIALTAR SEALADAC NA HÉIREANN - overprint on stamps of Great Britain - *Ireland*

RIAU - overprint on stamps of Indonesia or Netherlands Indies - *Indonesia*, Riouw Archipelago

RICEVUTA - *Italy, Somalia* or *San Marino*, parcel post

RIEL - (monetary unit) - *Cambodia*

RIGSBANK SKILLING - (monetary unit) - *Denmark*

R.I.IRAN - *Iran*

RIN - (monetary unit) - *Japan*

RIO DE ORO - overprint on stamp inscribed "Territorios Españoles del Africa Occidental" - *Rio De Oro*

R I S - overprint on Netherlands Indies stamp inscribed "Indonesia" - *Indonesia*

RIVERS - overprint on diagonally cut bisect stamp - *Niger Coast Protectorate*

RIZEH - overprint on stamps of Russia - *Russia*, Offices in Turkey

RL.PLATA F - (monetary unit) - *Cuba* or *Philippines*

RN. - (monetary unit) - *Japan*

R.O. - overprint on stamps of Turkey - *Eastern Rumelia*

ROAVOAMENA - *Madagascar* local

ROBERTSPORT - with no country name - *Liberia*, registry stamp

R.O.DEL URUGUAY - *Uruguay*

RODI - alone or as overprint on stamps of Italy - *Italy*, Aegean Islands, Rhodes

ROMAGNE - *Italian States*, Romagna (one of the Papal States)

ROMAN STATES - *Italian States*, Roman States

ROMANA or **ROMINA** - *Romania*

ROMANA with **"ZONA DE OCUPATIE"** - overprint on stamps of Hungary - *Hungary*, Romanian occupation

ROSS DEPENDENCY - *New Zealand*, Ross Dependency

ROSSIJA - *Russia* former republic of the U.S.S.R.

ROUAD - overprint on stamps of French Offices in the Levant - *Rouad*

ROUMELIE ORIENTALE - overprint on stamps of Turkey - *Eastern Rumelia*

ROYAUME "ALMOUTAWAKKILIYYAH" du YEMEN - *Yemen*

ROYAUME DE L'ARABIE S(A)OUDITE - *Saudi Arabia*

ROYAUME D'EGYPTE - *Egypt*

ROYAUME DE YEMEN - *Yemen*

ROYAUME Others - see name after "Royaume (du)"

RP - (monetary unit - rappen) - *Liechtenstein* or *Switzerland*

RPE SHQIPERISE - *Albania*

R.P. KAMPUCHEA - *Cambodia*

R.P. ROMINA - *Romania*

RSA - *South Africa*

RSM or **R. SAN MARINO** - *San Marino*

RUANDA - overprint on stamps of Belgian Congo - *German East Africa*, Belgian occupation

RUANDA URUNDI - alone or as overprint on stamps of Belgian Congo - *Ruanda-Urundi*

RUMANIEN - overprint on stamps of Germany or Romania - *Romania*, German occupation

RUPEE - (monetary unit) - *Burma, India, Mesopotamia* and *Pakistan*
- surcharge on stamps of Japan - *Burma*, Japanese occupation
- overprint on stamps of Great Britain - *Oman*, Muscat

Ruffifch Polen - overprint in Germanic type on Germany - *Poland*, German occupation

RWANDAISE - *Rwanda*

RYUKYUS - *Ryukyu Islands*

- S -

S - (may have star and crescent in circle) - overprint on stamps of Straits Settlements - *Malaya*, Selangor

S.A. or **S.A.K.** - *Saudi Arabia*

SAAR, SAARGEBIET, SAARLAND, SAARLUFTPOST or **SAARPOST** - alone or as overprint on stamps of Germany - *Saar*

SABAH - on stamps inscribed "Malaysia" or as overprint on stamps of North Borneo - *Sabah* (Federation of Malaya)

SACHSEN - *German States*, Saxony
- with "Bundesland" - *Germany*, Russian Zone of Saxony

SAGGIO - overprint on stamps of Italy or Italian colonies means "Specimen"

SAHARA (ESPAÑOL or **OCCIDENTAL)** - alone or as overprint on stamps of Spain - *Spanish Sahara*

SAHARA OCCIDENTAL LA AGUERA - *Aguera (La)*

SAINT CHRISTOPHER, NEVIS, ANGUILLA - *St. Kitts-Nevis*

SAINT PIERRE ET MIQUELON - alone or as overprint on stamps of France - *St. Pierre and Miquelon*

SALONICCO - overprint on stamps of Italy - *Italy*, Offices in Turkey - Salonika

SALONIQUE - overprint on stamps of Russia - *Russia*, Offices in Turkey

SAMOA - alone or as overprint on stamps of Germany or New Zealand - *Samoa* or *Samoa (British)*

SAMOA I SISIFO - *Samoa* (listed with British Samoa by Scott)

SAMORZAD WARWISZKI - overprint on stamps of Poland - *South Lithuania*, Polish occupation (not listed by Scott)

SANDA - Scotland, local label

SANDJAK D'ALEXANDRETTE - overprint on stamps of Syria - *Alexandretta*

SANS DINERO - fantasy country

SANTANDER - *Colombia*, Santander Department

SAORSTAT EIREANN - overprint on stamps of Great Britain - *Ireland*

SAO TOME E PRINCIPE - *St. Thomas and Prince Islands*

S.A.R. - *Syria*

SARAWAK - on stamps inscribed "Malaysia" - *Sarawak*

SARK - *Guernsey* private local issue

SARKARI - *India*, Soruth feudatory state

SARRE - overprint on stamps of Bavaria or Germany - *Saar*

SASENO - overprint on stamps of Italy - *Saseno*

SATANG - (monetary unit) - *Thailand*

SAURASHTRA - alone or as overprint on stamp inscribed "Bhavnagar Durbar" - *India*, Soruth, feudatory state

SCADTA - *Colombia* airmail

SCARPANTO - overprint on stamps of Italy - *Italy*, Aegean Islands - Scarpanto

SCH(ILLING)(E) - (monetary unit) - *German States*

SCHLESWIG (HOLSTEIN) - *German States*, Schleswig Holstein

SCINDE DISTRICT DAWK - *India*, Scinde District post

SCUDO - (monetary unit) - *Italian States*, Roman States

SCUTARI DI ALBANIA - overprint on stamps of Italy - *Italy*, Offices in Turkey - Scutari

SEALAND - fantasy country

SEDANG - Indochina, non-postal label

SEGNATASSE (or **A**) - Italy and colonies, San Marino or Vatican City - postage due

SEIYUN - *Aden* , Kathiri State of Seiyun (Some issues are not listed.)

SEJM WILNIE - *Central Lithuania*

SELANGOR - *Malaya* or *Malaysia*, Selangor

SELANTAN - South Moluccas, unrecognized issue

SELLO 10° A.ˢ 1896Y97 - *Fernando Po*, revenue (some overprinted for postage)

SEN - (monetary unit) - Indonesia, Japan, Malaya, Ryukyu Islands or West Irian

SENEGAL - overprint on stamps of French Colonies - *Senegal*
- with surcharge - *Senegal* or *French West Africa*

SENEGAMBIE ET NIGER - *Senegambia and Niger*

SERBES - overprint on stamps of France - *Serbia*

SERBIEN - overprint on stamps of Bosnia and Herzegovina - *Serbia*, Austrian occupation- overprint on stamps of Yugoslavia - *Serbia*, German occupation

SERVICE (POSTAGE) - no country name - *India* or *Pakistan*

SERVICIO BOLIVARIANO DE TRANSPORTES AEREOS - *Colombia* airmail
- with "Ecuador" - *Ecuador* airmail

SERVICIO DE TRANSPORTES AEREOS EN COLOMBIA - *Colombia* airmail

SERVICIO POSTAL MEXICANA - *Mexico* Official

SEVILLA - overprint on stamps of Spain - *Spain*, Seville issue

SEVILLA - BARCELONA - *Spain*

S.GR. - (monetary unit) - *German States*

S H - in upper corners - *German States*, Schleswig Holstein

SHAHI - (monetary unit) - *Afghanistan* and *Iran*

SHANGHAI - overprint on stamps of the United States - *United States*, Offices in China

SHANGHAI L.P.O. or **SHANGHAI MUNICIPALITY** - *Shanghai*

SHARJAH & DEPENDENCIES - *Sharjah* (many not listed by Scott)

S H C O - in corners of shield - *Mozambique* postal tax

SHEKEL - (monetary unit) - *Israel*

SHIHR AND MUKALLA - Aden locals

SHQIPENIA, SHQIPENIE, SHQIPERIA, SHQIPERIJA, SHQIPERISE, SHQIPNI, SHQIPNIJA, SHQIPONIES, SHQIPTARI or **SHQYPTARE**
- alone or as overprint on stamps of Turkey - *Albania*

S.H.S. - overprint on stamps of Bosnia & Herzegovina or Hungary - *Yugoslavia*

SHUNA - publicity label (Great Britain)

SIAM - *Thailand*

SICILIA - *Italian States*, Two Sicilies

SIEGE OF MAFEKING - *Cape of Good Hope*

SIGILLUM NOV CAMB AUST - *New South Wales*

SILB. GR. (or **GROSCH.**) - (monetary unit) - *German States*

SIMI - overprint on stamps of Italy - *Italy*, Aegean Islands, Simi

SINGAPORE MALAYA - *Singapore*

SIN VALOR POSTAL - Spain charity labels

SIRMOOR - *India*, Sirmoor feudatory state

SIROTAM - surcharge on stamps of Italy - *Yugoslavia*, German occupation of Ljubljana

SKILL(ING) - (monetary unit) - Denmark, Iceland, Norway and Sweden

SLD. - (monetary unit - soldi) - *Austria*, Offices in Turkey

SLESVIG - *Schleswig*

SILBER GR. - (monetary unit) - *German States*

SLOVENIJA - *Slovenia*, formerly part of Yugoslavia

SLOVENSKA POSTA - *Czechoslovakia*, Slovakia

SLOVENSKO - *Czechoslovakia*, Slovakia

SLOVENSKO - overprint on stamps of Hungary - unofficial issue

SLOVENSKO PRIMORIE - with "Istria" - *Yugoslavia*, issues for Istria and the Slovene Coast

SLOVENSKY STAT - overprint on stamps of Czechoslovakia - *Czechoslovakia*, Slovakia

SLOV.LIGA.SLOVENSKY BRAT. OBJIM SI MAT. - Slovakian label issued in the United States

S.MARINO - *San Marino*

SMIRNE - overprint on stamps of Italy - *Italy*, Offices in Turkey - Smyrna

S.M.O.M. - Knights of Malta, stamps not recognized by the Universal Postal Union

SMYRN(E) - overprint on stamps of Russia - *Russia*, Offices in Turkey

SN. - (monetary unit) - *Japan* or *Ryukyu Islands*

S.O.1920 - overprint on stamps of Czechoslovakia or Poland - *Eastern Silesia*

SOAY - publicity label, Great Britain

SOBRE CUOTA PARA BULTOS POSTALES - *Mexico* parcel post

SOBREPORTE - *Colombia* airmail or postage due

SOBRETASA AEREA - *Colombia* airmail

SOCIALIST PEOPLE'S LIBYAN ARAB JAMAHIRIYA - *Libya*

SOCIEDAD COLOMBO-ALEMANA DE TRANSPORTES AEREOS - *Colombia*

SOCIEDADE DE GEOGRAPHIA DE LISBOA - *Portugal*, franchise stamp

SOCIEDADE HUMANITARIA CRUZ DO ORIENTE - *Mozambique* postal tax

SOCIEDADE PORTUGUEZA DA CRUZ VERMELHA - *Portugal*, franchise

SOCIÉTÉ DES NATIONS - overprint on stamps of Switzerland - *Switzerland*, Officials for the League of Nations

SOL - (monetary unit) - *Peru*

SOLDI - (monetary unit) - *Austria*, Lombardy Venetia or *Italian States*, Tuscany

SOLIDARITÉ FRANÇAISE - *French Colonies* semipostal

SOMALIA (ITALIANA) - alone or as overprint on stamps of Italy - *Somalia*

SOMALI DEMOCRATIC REPUBLIC - *Somalia*

SOMALILAND PROTECTORATE - (British) *Somaliland Protectorate*

SOMALIS - *Somali Coast*

SOM UBESORGET or **SOM UINDLOST** - *Norway*, returned letter stamp

SONORA - *Mexico*, civil war issue

SOMALIYA, SOOMAALIYA or **SOOMAALIYEED** - *Somalia*

SORUTH - *India*, Soruth, feudatory state

SOSNOWICE - Poland local

SOUDAN - overprint on stamps of Egypt - *Sudan*

SOUDAN (FRANÇAIS) - alone or as overprint on stamps of French Colonies or Upper Senegal and Niger - *French Sudan*

SOURASHTRA - *India*, Soruth feudatory state

SOUTH ARABIA - with "Federation of" - *South Arabia*, British Dependency

    - overprint on stamps of Aden - Kathiri State of Seiyun, Qu'aiti State in Hadhramaut or Mahra State - not recognized

    - State of Upper Yafa - not recognized

SOUTHERN RHODESIA - overprint on stamps of Great Britain - *Southern Rhodesia* postage due

SOUTHERN YEMEN - alone or as overprint on stamps of South Arabia - *Yemen*, People's Democratic Republic

SOUTH GEORGIA - alone *South Georgia* (British)

SOUTH GEORGIA AND THE SOUTH SANDWICH IS(LANDS) - *Falkland Islands Dependencies*

SOUTH GEORGIA DEPENDENCY OF - *Falkland Islands Dependencies*

SOUTH KASAI - alone or as overprint on stamps of Congo - not recognized

SOUTH ORKNEYS DEPENDENCY OF - *Falkland Islands Dependencies*

SOUTH SHETLANDS DEPENDENCY OF - *Falkland Islands Dependencies*

SOUTH WEST AFRICA - overprint on stamps of South Africa - *South West Africa*

SOVRANO MILITARE ORDINE DI MALTA - local issue of Malta

SOWJETISCHE BESATZUNGS ZONE - overprint on stamps of Germany - *Germany*, Russian occupation

S P - intertwined as a monogram - *Colombia*, Cauca Department

SPITZBERGEN - *Norway*, locals or publicity labels

S P M - overprint on stamps of French Colonies - *St. Pierre & Miquelon*

SPOORWEGEN - *Belgium* parcel post

S.Q.TRSTA.VUJA - *Yugoslavia*, Trieste

SRODKOWA LITWA - *Central Lithuania*

ST or **STG** - (monetary unit) - *Thailand*

STADT BERLIN - *Germany*, Russian Zone of Berlin (Those without overprint "Sowjetische Besatzungs Zone" are Russian issues for Berlin - Brandenburg.)

STADT-POST-BASEL - *Switzerland*, Basel Canton

STADT STRAUSBERG - *Germany* World War II local

STAFFA - Scotland, publicity label

STAMP - only English inscription - *Tibet* official

STAMPALIA - overprint on stamps of Italy - *Italy*, Aegean Islands - Stampalia

STATE OF NORTH BORNEO - *North Borneo* (British)

STATE OF OMAN - labels ("Sultanate of Oman" is legitimate)

STATE OF SINGAPORE - *Singapore*

STATI PARM(ENSI) - *Italian States*, Parma

ST. CHRISTOPHER AND NEVIS - *St. Kitts-Nevis*

ST. CHRISTOPHER-NEVIS-ANGUILLA - *St. Kitts-Nevis*

STEEP HOLM - Great Britain, publicity label

STELLALAND - *South Africa*, Stellaland

STEMPEL - with "centes" - *Austria*, Lombardy Venetia
    - with "kreuzers" - *Austria*

S. THOME (or **TOME**) **E. PRINCIPE** - *St. Thomas & Prince Islands*

ST KILDA - private local issue, Great Britain

STOCKHOLM 1924 - *Sweden*

ST. PIERRE M-ON - overprint on stamps of French Colonies - *St. Pierre & Miquelon*

STRAITS SETTLEMENTS - alone, with "Malaya" or as overprint on stamps of Labuan - *Straits Settlements*

STROMA - publicity label, Great Britain

S.T.T. (or **S.T.TRSTA**) **VUJ(N)A** - alone or as overprint on stamps of Yugoslavia -
Yugoslavia, Trieste

S.U., **SU** in circle with star and crescent or **S. UJONG** - overprint on stamps of Straits Settlements - *Malaya*, Sungei Ujong

SUBMARINO CORREO - *Spain*, submarine mail

SUCRE - (monetary unit) - *Ecuador*

SUD KASAI - South Kasai, part of Congo - not recognized

SUID AFRIKA - *South Africa*

SUIDWES AFRIKA - alone or as overprint on stamps of South Africa - *South West Africa*

SUL BOLLETTINO or **SULLA RICEVUTA** - *Italy* or Italian Colonies
    - on stamps with star and crescent or Arabic writing - *Somalia*

SULTANAT D'ANJOUAN - *Anjouan*

SULTANATE OF OMAN - *Oman*

SUMMER ISLES - private local issue, Great Britain

SUNGEI UJONG - overprint on stamps of Straits Settlements - *Malaya*, Sungei Ujong

SUOMI* - *Finland*

SURINAME* - *Surinam*

SVARSLOSEN - *Sweden*, reply paid stamps

SVERIGE* - *Sweden*

SVENDBORG - *Denmark* local

SWA - alone or as overprint on stamps of South Africa - *South West Africa*

SWAZI(E)LAND - overprint on stamps of Transvaal or South Africa - *Swaziland*

SYRIAN ARAB REPUBLIC - *Syria*

SYRIE(NNE) or **SYRIE** - **GRAND LIBAN** - alone or as overprint on stamps of France - *Syria*

- T -

T - overprint in circle on stamps of Peru - Peru, Huacho provisional
    - in each corner of stamp - Dominican Republic postage due
    - with monetary unit "F" and heraldic lion - Belgium postage due

TABORA - overprint on stamps of Belgian Congo - not authorized

TACNA Y ARICA - Peru, postal tax

TAHITI - overprint on stamps of French Colonies or French Polynesia
    - Tahiti

TAJIKISTAN - Formerly Tadhikistan in U.S.S.R.

TAKCA - Bulgaria, postage due

TAKSÉ - Albania, postage due

TALCA - Chile, Talca postal tax

TAMMERFORS - Finland local

TANGA - (monetary unit) - Portuguese India

TANGANYIKA KENYA UGANDA - Kenya, Uganda, Tanzania

TANGANYIKA & ZANZIBAR - Tanzania

TANGER - alone or as overprint on stamps of Spain - Spanish Morocco, Tangiers
- overprint on stamps of France - France, Offices in Morocco

TANGER ELKSAR - Morocco local

TANGER-FEZ - Morocco local

TANGIER - overprint on stamps of Great Britain - *Great Britain*, Offices in Morocco

TANGIER-MOROCCO-LARAICHE - Morocco local

TANZANIA - with "Muungano" - *Zanzibar*

TANZANIA UGANDA KENYA - *Kenya, Uganda, Tanzania*

TASSA GAZZETTE - *Italian States*, Modena, newspaper tax

TATI CONCESSIONS - South Africa local

TAXA DE GUERRA - values in avos - *Macao* or *Timor*
- values in 0$ - *Portuguese Africa*
- values in RP - *Portuguese India*
- values in reis - *Portuguese Guinea*

TAXA DEVIDA - *Brazil*, postage due

T^{bre} MOVIL F^{do} P^{oo} - Fernando Po, revenues, some overprinted for postal use

T.C. - overprint on stamps of India, Cochin - *India*, Travancore - Cochin

TCHAD - overprint on stamps of Middle Congo - *Chad*

TCHONGKING - overprint on stamps of Indochina - *France*, Offices in China - Tchongking

T.C.POSTALARI - Turkey

TE BETALEN - preceded by "A Payer" - *Belgium*, postage due

TE BETALEN PORT - alone or as overprint - *Netherlands, Netherlands Antilles, Netherlands Indies* or *Surinam*

TELEGRAFOS - Philippines, telegraph stamps, some made valid for postage by "Habititado" overprint

T.E.O. - overprint on stamps of France, Offices in Turkey - *Cilicia*
- overprint on stamps of France or French Offices in Turkey, with values in milliemes or piastres - *Syria*

T.E.O. CILICIE - overprint on stamps of Turkey - *Cilicia*

TERRES AUSTRALES ET ANTARCTIQUES FRANÇAISES - alone or as overprint on stamps of Madagascar - *French Southern and Antarctic Territories*

TERRITOIRE DE L'ININI - overprint on stamps of French Guiana - *Inini*

TERRITOIRE DU FEZZAN - *Libya*, French occupation of Fezzan

TERRITOIRE DU NIGER - overprint on stamps of Upper Senegal and Niger - *Niger*

TERRITOIRE FRANÇAIS DES AFARS ET DES ISSAS - *Afars and Issas*

TERRITOIRE MILITAIRE FEZZAN - *Libya*, French occupation of Fezzan

TERRITORIO DE IFNI - overprint on stamps of Spain - *Ifni*

Alphabetical listing of stamp inscriptions

TERRITORIOS DEL AFRICA OCCIDENTAL ESPAÑOLA - *Spanish West Africa*

TERRITORIOS (or TERRS.) ESPAÑOLES DEL GOLFO DE GUINEA - alone or as overprint on stamps of Spain - *Spanish Guinea*

TETE - alone or as overprint on stamps of Macao, Portuguese Africa or Timor - *Tete*

TETOUAN MAROC CHECHOUAN - Morocco local

TETUAN - overprint on stamps of Spain or Spanish Morocco - *Tetuan*

TETUAN-SHESHUAN - Morocco local

THAI - *Thailand*

THAILAND - with value in cents - *Malaya*, Thai occupation

THE GAMBIA - Gambia

THE GILBERT ISLANDS - overprint on stamps of Gilbert and Ellice Islands - *Gilbert Islands*

THERESIENSTADT - concentration camp label

THIRTY TWO CENTS - with picture of ship - *Liberia*

THOMOND - Ireland, fantasy label

THRACE INTERALLIEE (or OCCIDENTALE) - overprint on stamps of Bulgaria - *Thrace*, Allied occupation

THRONDHJEMS (or TRONDHJEMS) BYPOST - Norway, local

THULE - Greenland, local

THÜRINGEN - Germany, Russian Zone - *Thuringia*

THURN UND TAXIS - *German States*, Thurn & Taxis

TICAL - (monetary unit) - *Thailand*

TIENTSIN - overprint on stamps of Italy - *Italy*, Offices in China

TIERRA DEL FUEGO - Argentina local

TIMBRE IMPERIAL JOURNAUX - *France*, newspaper stamp

TIMBRE MOVIL - *Spain*, tax stamp, some authorized for postal use

TIMBRE POSTE - overprint on stamps of France postage due - *French Morocco*, French Offices in Morocco

TIMBRE TAXE - with numeral and no country name - *French Colonies*, general issue postage due

TIMBRUL AVIATIEI - *Romania*, postal tax

TIMOR - overprint on stamps of Macao or surcharge on stamps of Mozambique - *Timor*

TIMOR PORTUGUES - *Timor*

TIN CAN ISLAND - see Niuafo'ou listing

TJÄNSTE or TJENSTE FRIMARKE - *Sweden* Official

TJEDAN SOLIDARNOSTI - *Yugoslavia*, postal tax

TJENESTEFRIMERKE - *Norway* Official

TJENESTE POST FRIMAERKE - *Denmark* Official

TOGA - *Tonga*

TOGO - alone or as overprint on stamps of Germany or Dahomey - *Togo*

TOGO ANGLO-FRENCH OCCUPATION - overprint on stamps of German Togo or Gold Coast - *Togo* (British)

TOGO Occupation franco anglaise - overprint on stamps of German Togo or Dahomey - *Togo*, French occupation

TOGOLAISE - *Togo*

TOKELAU ISLANDS - alone or as overprint on stamps of New Zealand - *Tokelau Islands*

TOLIMA - *Colombia*, Tolima Department

TOMAN - (monetary unit) - *Iran*

TONSBERG - Norway local

TO PAY - *Great Britain*, postage due

TOSCANO - *Italian States*, Tuscany

TOU - (monetary unit) - *Iran*

TOUVA or **TOVVA** - *Tannu Tuva* (Those with "Posta Touva" are not listed.)

TRAITE DE VERSAILLES - overprint on stamps of Germany - *Allenstein*

TRANS-JORDAN - Jordan

TRANSKEI - *South Africa*, Transkei native homeland

TRANSPORTO PACCHI IN CONCESSIONE - *Italy*, parcel post authorized delivery

TRAVANCORE-ANCHEL (or **ANCHAL**) - *India*, Travancore or Travancore - Cochin

TRAVANCORE-COCHIN - *India*, Travancore - Cochin feudatory state

TREBIZONDE - overprint on stamps of Russia - *Russia*, Offices in Turkey

TRENGGANU - *Malaya* or *Malaysia*, Trengganu State

TRENTINO - overprint on stamps of Austria - *Austria*, Italian occupation

TRIDENTINA - overprint on stamps of Italy - *Austria*, Italian occupation

TRIESTE - overprint on stamps of Italy - *Italy*, Trieste

TRIPOLI - preceded by "Fiera Campionaria" - *Libya*

TRIPOLI DI BARBERIA - overprint on stamps of Italy - *Italy*, Offices in Africa - Tripoli

TRIPOLI MAGGIO 1934 - overprint on stamps of Libya - *Tripolitania*

TRIPOLITANIA - alone or as overprint on stamps of Italy - *Tripolitania*

TRISTAN DA CUNHA - overprint on stamps of St. Helena - *Tristan Da Cunha*

TROMSO BYPOST - Norway local

T.Ta. C. - *Turkey*, postal tax

TUMACO - *Colombia*, Cauca provisional

TUNIS, TUNISIE or **TUNISIENNE** - *Tunisia*

TÜRK(IYE) (CÜMHURIYETI) (POSTALARI) - *Turkey*

TÜRKIYE COCUK ESIRGEME KORUMU or **KIZILAY CEMIYETI** - *Turkey*, postal tax

TURKMENISTAN - formerly Turkmenia in U.S.S.R.

TUVALU - overprint on stamps of Gilbert and Ellice Islands - *Tuvalu*

TWO PENCE - with no country name and queen on throne above inscription - *Victoria*

- U -

U.A.E. - alone or as overprint on stamps of Abu Dhabi - *United Arab Emirates*

U.A.EMIRATES - *United Arab Emirates*

U. A. R. - United Arab Republic - "M" or "E" values - *Egypt* - "P" values - *Syria*

U.C.CO. - Canada, Upper Columbia Company local

UCIA - on vertically cut bisect stamp - *St. Lucia*

UDINE - Italy, local

UG - typewritten with numeral - *Uganda*

UGANDA - overprint on stamps of British East Africa - *Uganda*

UGANDA KENYA TANGANYIKA (ZANZIBAR) - *Kenya, Uganda and Tanzania*

UGANDA PROTECTORATE - *Uganda*

UKRAINE - overprint on stamps of Germany - *Russia*, German occupation

U.K.T.T. - overprint with "Cameroons" on Nigeria - *Cameroons* (British)

UKU LETA - United States, Hawaii

ULTRAMAR - with year date - *Cuba* or *Puerto Rico* (some used in Philippines)

- with values in "Avos"or "Reis" - *Macao* or *Portuguese Guinea*

UNIE VAN ZUID AFRIKA - *South Africa*

UNION FRANÇAISE ROYAUME DU LAOS - *Laos*

UNION ISLAND - *St. Vincent Grenadines*, Union Island

UNION OF SOUTH AFRICA - *South Africa*

UNION POSTAL ARABE - *Libya*

UNION POSTAL UNIVERSELLE EQUATEUR - *Ecuador*

UNITED ARAB REPUBLIC - *Egypt* or *Syria* (see U.A.R. above)

UNITED REPUBLIC OF TANGANYIKA & ZANZIBAR - *Tanzania*

UNIVERSAL POSTAL UNION 1874-1949 - with king and crown - *Great Britain*

UNTEA - overprint on stamps of Netherlands New Guinea - *West Irian* (West New Guinea)

UPPER YAFA - South Arabia or Yemen locals

U.P.U. - Universal Postal Union - commemorated by many countries

U.R.I. - overprint on Yugoslavia semipostal - stamp had no official postal value

URUNDI - overprint on stamps of Belgian Congo - *German East Africa*, Belgian occupation

USKUB - overprint on stamps of Turkey - *Turkey*

USSR - Russia

USTC - overprint on stamps ofIndia-Cochin - *India* - Travancore-Cochin

UTAH - U.S. bogus issue

- V -

VADSO - Norway local

VALENCIA - with "Plan Sur de" - *Spain*, obligatory tax stamp

VALLEES D'ANDORRE - *Andorra*, French administration

VALONA - overprint on stamps of Italy - *Italy*, Offices in Turkey

VALPARAISO MULTADA - *Chile*, postage due

VANCOUVER('S) ISLAND - *British Columbia and Vancouver Island*

VAN DIEMEN'S LAND - *Tasmania*

VARDO BYPOST - Norway local

VARIG - Brazil, private airmail carrier

VATHY - overprint on stamps of France - *France*, Offices in Turkey

VATICANA(or **E**) - *Vatican City*

VEILE BYPOST - Denmark local

VENDA - *South Africa*, Venda native homeland

VENEZA, **VENEZOLANA**, **VENEZOLANO** or **VENZ**. - *Venezuela*

VENEZIA GIULIA or **TRIDENTINA** - overprint on stamps of Austria or Italy - *Austria*, Italian occupation

VEREINTE NATIONEN - *United Nations*, Offices in Vienna

VETEKEVERRIA E MIRDITES - *Albania*, unauthorized

VIBORG BYPOST - Denmark local

VICTORIA LAND - overprint on stamps of New Zealand - New Zealand, Scott South Pole Expedition, not considered regular postage

VIET NAM - overprint on stamps of Indochina - not valid

VIET NAM (CONG HOA) - *Viet Nam* (South)

VIET NAM DAN CHU CONG HOA - *Viet Nam* (North)

VII CONGRESSO UPU - *Spain*

VOJNA UPRAVA JUGOSLAVENSKE ARMIJE - overprint on stamps of Yugoslavia - *Yugoslavia*, issues for Istria and the Slovene Coast

VOJSKO or **VOJENSKA POSTA** - *Czechoslovakia*, Legion Post in Siberia

VOLK∫TAAT BAYERN - *German States*, Bavaria

VOM EMPFANGER EINZUZIEHEN - *Danzig*, postage due

VOM EMPFANGER ZAHLBAR - *German States*, Bavaria, postage due

V.R. SPECIAL POST - overprint on stamps of Transvaal - *Cape of Good Hope*, British occupation

V.R. TRANSVAAL - overprint on stamps of Transvaal - *Transvaal*, British occupation

VUJ(N)A STT - alone or as overprint on stamps of Yugoslavia - *Yugoslavia*, Trieste

- W -

WADHWAN - *India*, Wadhwan feudatory state

WALLIS ET FUTUNA - alone or as overprint on stamps of New Caledonia - *Wallis & Futuna Islands*

WARSZAWA - Poland, local Warsaw post
- with "Poczta Polska" overprint - *Poland*

WEIHNACHTEN 1944 - overprint on stamps of Italy, Aegean Islands - Rhodes - unauthorized German overprint

WENDEN or **WENDENSCHE(N) (KREIS)** - *Russia*, former province of Wenden

W. (or **WEST**) **AUSTRALIA** - *Western Australia*

WESTERN SAMOA - alone or as overprint on stamps of New Zealand - *Samoa* (British)

WESTUNGARN ORGLAND - overprint on stamps of Hungary - Western Hungary (not listed by Scott)

WINTERHILFE - surcharge on stamps of Italy - *Yugoslavia*, German occupation of Ljubljana

WN, **WON** or **WUN** - (monetary unit) - *Korea*

WÜRTTEMBERG - *German States*, Württemberg
- *Germany*, Württemberg, French occupation

- X - Y -

XEIMAPPA - part of overprint on stamps of Greece - *Epirus*

Y.A.R. - *Yemen* (Arab Republic)

YCA - overprint on stamps of Peru - *Peru*, Yca provisional

Y.C.P.P. - *Ukraine*

YCTAB 1905 - *Montenegro*

YEMEN ARAB REPUBLIC - *Yemen*

YEMEN PDR - *Yemen People's Democratic Republic*

YEN or **YN** - (monetary unit) - *Japan, Manchukuo* or *Ryukyu Islands*

YIL DONUMU - *Turkey*, postal tax

YKPAIHCbKA - *Ukraine*

YKP. H. P. or **YKP. H. PEII** - overprint on stamps of Austria or Bosnia & Herzegovina - *Western Ukraine*

YKSI MARKKA - *Finland*

YUNNAN-FOU or **YUNNAN SEN** - overprint on stamps of Indochina - *France*, Offices in China

- Z -

Z - fancy monogram overprint on stamps of Russia - *Armenia*
- with additional star overprint - *Transcaucasian Federated Republics*

Z. AFR. REP(UBLIEK) - *Transvaal*

ZAIRE or **ZAJRE** - *Zaire*

ZALOTKOP - *Poland*, under Russian dominion

ZANZIBAR - alone on French type stamps or as overprint on stamps of France - *France*, Offices in Zanzibar
- alone or as overprint on stamps of British East Africa or India - *Zanzibar*

ZANZIBAR-TANZANIA - *Zanzibar*

ZARKACK - Poland, Zarki local

ZARSKA BULGARSKA POSTA - Royalist Bulgaria Government in Exile labels

ZAWIERCIE - Poland local

ZEGELREGT - Transvaal revenue

ZEITUNGS - *Austria*, newspaper stamp

ZELAYA - *Nicaragua*, Zelaya Province

ZENTRALER KURIERDIENST - *German Democratic Republic* Official

ZIL (or **ZES**) **ELWAGNE** (or **ELOIGNE** or **ELWANNYEN**) **SESEL** - Seychelles - not listed by Scott

ZIMSKA POMOC - with "Winterhilfe" - overprint on stamps of Italy - *Yugoslavia*, German occupation of Ljubljana

ZLOTE or **ZLOTY** - (monetary unit) - *Poland*

ZONA DE OCUPATIE ROMANA - overprint on stamps of Hungary - *Hungary*, Romanian occupation

ZONA OCCUPATA FIUMANO KUPA - overprint on stamps of Yugoslavia - *Yugoslavia*, Italian occupation

ZONA (DE) PROTECTORADO ESPAÑOL - alone or as overprint on stamps of Spain - *Spanish Morocco*

ZONE FRANÇAISE - *Germany*, French occupation

ZRACNA POSTA - *Yugoslavia*, Trieste, military government issue

Z.S.G.T. - Hungary local

ZUID AFRIKA - *South Africa*

ZUID AFRIKANAASCHE REPUBLIEK - *Transvaal*

ZUID-WEST AFRIKA - overprint on stamps of South Africa - *South West*

Africa
ZULULAND - overprint on stamps of Great Britain or Natal - *Zululand*
Z.u.n.Z. - *Armenia*
ZURICH - *Switzerland*, Zurich Canton

- OTHER -
1898 - 1923 - *Netherlands*
"5" - overprint on stamps of French Colonies with or without "C.CH." - *Cochin China*
Stamps of India surcharged with crown and new value in cents - *Straits Settlements*

- GREEK -
ΑΝΑΤΟΛΙΚΗ ΡΩΜΥΛΙΑ - with "Emp. Ottoman" - *Eastern Rumelia*
ΑΥΤΟΝΟΜΟΣ - Epirus
Β.ΗΠΕΙΡΟΣ - overprint on stamps of Greece - *Epirus*, Greek occupation
ΒΟΗΘΕΙΤΕ - Greece
ΔΡΑΧ(ΜΑΙ) - (monetary unit) - *Greece*
ΕΛΛ., ΕΛΛΑC or ΕΛΛΑΣ* - "Hellas" - *Greece*
    - overprint on stamps of Italy - *Ionian Islands*, Greek occupation
    - overprint on stamps of Crete - *Crete*
Ε*Δ or Ε*Λ - *Greece*, Aegean Islands - Chios
ΕΛΛΗΝΙΚΗ ΔΙΟΙΚΗΣΙΣ - overprint on stamps of Greece or Bulgaria - *Greece*, occupation and annexation stamps
ΕΛΛΗΝΙΚΗ ΔΗΜΟΚΡΑΤΙΑ - *Greece*
ΕΛΛΗΝΙΚΗ ΚΑΤ°ΧΗ ΛΕΠΤΑ.50 - overprint on stamps of Turkey - *Turkey in Asia*, private issue
ΕΛΛΗΝΙΚΗ 1914 ΧΕΙΜΑΡΡΑ - overprint on stamps of Greece - *Epirus*
ΕΝΑΡΙΘΜΟΝ ΓΡΑΜΜΑΤΟΣΗΜΟΝ - *Greece*, postage due
    - with airplane overprint - *Greece*, airmail
ΕΝΑΕΡ. ΤΑΧΥΔΡ. ΣΥΓΚΟΙΝ - *Greece*, airmail
ΕΘΝΙΚΗ ΠΕΡΙΘΑΛΨΙΣ - *Greece*, postal tax
ΗΠΕΙΡΟΣ - *Epirus*
ΗΡΑΚΛΕΙΟΥ - *Crete*, British sphere, Heraklion District
ΙΚΑΡΙΑΣ - *Greece*, Aegean Islands, Icaria
ΙΟΝΙΚΟΝ ΚΡΑΤΟΣ - *Ionian Islands*, British protectorate
ΛΕΠΤΑ, ΛΕΠΤΟΝ, ΛΕΓΤΑ or ΛΕΓΤΟΝ - (monetary unit) - *Crete*, *Epirus*, *Greece* or *Thrace*
ΛΗΜΝΟΣ - overprint on stamps of Greece - *Greece*, Aegean Islands - Lemnos
ΟΛΥΜ., ΟΛΥΜΙ ΙΑΚΟΙ or ΟΛΥΜΓ. ΑΓΩΝΕΣ - *Greece*
ΦΥΜΑΤΙΚΩΝ Τ.Τ.Τ. - *Greece*
ΦΥΜ. Τ.Τ.Τ. - *Greece*, postal tax
ΠΡΟΣΩΠΙΚΟΥ Τ.Τ.Τ. - *Greece*, postal tax
ΠΡΟΣΩΡΙΝΟΝ ΤΑΧΥΔΡΟΜ(ΕΙΟΝ) ΗΡΑΚΛΕΙΟΥ - *Crete*, British sphere of administration
ΠΑΡΑΔΕΣ - (monetary unit) - *Crete*
ΣΑΜΟΥ - *Greece*, Aegean Islands, Samos
Σ.Δ.Δ. - overprint on Greece - *Greece*, for use in Dodecanese Islands
ΧΑΡΤΟΣΗΜΟΝ - Greece, revenues (some overprinted for use as postal tax stamps)

З.У.Н.Р. — overprint in corners on stamps of Austria - *Western Ukraine*

ЗСФСР — alone or as overprint (in star) on stamps of Russia - *Transcaucasian Federal Republic*

ЗGФGР — *Transcaucasian Federated Republic*

АСОБНЫ АТРАА — White Russia (propaganda labels)

АВИОПОЧТА — *Russia*

ДРЖАВА С.Х.С. — *Yugoslavia*, Bosnia & Herzegovina

АЗЄРБАИДЖАНСКАЯ — *Azerbaijan*

БЬПГАРСКА — *Bulgaria*

БАКУ — *Baku*

БАТУМ — *Batum*

БУЛГАРЙЯ — *Bulgaria*

БЬЛГАРИЯ* — *Bulgaria*

ВЕНДЕНСКАЯ — *Russia*, Wenden

ВОСТОЧНАЯ КОРРЕС ПОН ДЕНЦІЯ — *Russia*, Offices in Turkey

СРБЙJА, СРПСКА — *Serbia*

САНТИМ, САНТ — (monetary unit) — *Bulgaria*

САНАТОРИУМЬ — *Bulgaria*

СТОТИНКИ, СТ, СТОТ — (monetary unit) — *Bulgaria*

ЕДИНАЯ РОССІЯ — *South Russia*, Denikin issue

НРБЪЛГАРИЯ — *Bulgaria*

НОВЧ(ЙТ) — (monetary unit) — *Montenegro*

ФРАНКЬ — (monetary unit) — *Bulgaria*

JУГОСЛАВЙJА — alone or as overprint on stamps of Serbia — *Yugoslavia*

КАРПАТСЬКА-УКРАІНА — overprint on stamp inscribed Cesko-Slovensko — *Czechoslovakia*, Carpatho-Ukraine

КРАJЬЕВСТВО С.Х.С. — overprint on stamps of Bosnia & Herzegovina — *Yugoslavia*

К. СГБСКА — *Serbia*

КОН, КОП, КON — (monetary unit) — Batum, Far Eastern Republic, Finland, Latvia, Russia, South Russia

РОССІЯ — *Russia*, South Russia

РУВ or РУЬ — (monetary unit) — Finland, Russia, Serbia, South Russia overprint on stamps of Russia — *South Russia*

РУССКАЯ ПОУТА — overprint on stamps of Ukraine or Russia — *Russia*, Offices in Turkey
— Latvia, Russian occupation (never put into use)

Р.О.П.И.Т. — with no other lettering — *Russia*, Offices in Turkey, or *Ukraine*

ПАРА(Е) — (monetary unit) — *Montenegro* or *Serbia*

ПОЩТА — *Montenegro* or *Serbia*

ПОЧТА — "Postage" — *Russia*
— with "Post" — *Germany*, Soviet Zone (Saxony)

ПОЧТ МАРКА — *Azerbaijan*

ПОЧТОВАЯ МАРКА — *Far Eastern Republic, Finland, Russia, Serbia, South Russia*

ЦАРСТВО — *Bulgaria*

ЦОРТО СКРИСОРИ — *Romania*, Moldavia 1858 issue

ЦОРТО МАРКА — *Montenegro*

ЦРНА ГОРА — alone or as overprint on stamps of Italy — *Montenegro*

УКРАІНСЬКА — *Ukraine*

Alphabets

Greek

A	α	alpha
B	β	beta
Γ	γ	gamma
Δ	δ	delta
E	ε	epsilon
Z	ζ	zeta
H	η	eta
Θ	ϑ	theta
I	ι	iota
K	κ	kappa
Λ	λ	lambda
M	μ	mu
N	ν	nu
Ξ	ξ	xi
O	o	omicron
Π	π	pi
P	ρ	rho
Σ	σ	sigma
T	τ	tau
Υ	υ	upsilon
Φ	φ	phi
X	χ	chi
Ψ	ψ	psi
Ω	ω	omega

Cyrillic

А
Б
В
Г
Д
Е
Ё
Ж
З
И
Й
К
Л
М
Н
О
П
Р
С
Т
У
Ф
Х
Ц
Ч
Ш
Щ
Ъ
Ы
Ь
Э
Ю
Я

Alphabets

Hindi consonants

ka	क	na	न
kha	ख	pa	प
ga	ग	pha	फ
gha	घ	ba	ब
na	ङ	bha	भ
cha	च	ma	म
chha	छ	ya	य
ja	ज	ra	र
jha	झ	la	ल
na	ञ	va	व
ta	ट	sa	श
tha	ठ	sa	ष
da	ड	sa	स
dha	ढ	ha	ह
na	ण	m	.
ta	त	h	:
tha	थ	~	ँ
da	द	ra	ड़
dha	ध	rha	ढ़

Hindi vowels

a	अ	ri	ऋ
ā	आ	e,ē	ए
i	इ	oi,ai	ऐ
ī	ई	o,ō	ओ
u	उ	ou,au	औ
ū	ऊ		

Alphabets

Gujarati consonants

ka	ક	da	દ
kha	ખ	dha	ધ
ga	ગ	na	ન
gha	ઘ	pa	પ
na	ઙ	pha	ફ
cha	ચ	ba	બ
chha	છ	bha	ભ
ja	જ	ma	મ
jha	ઝ	ya	ય
na	ઞ	ra	ર
ta	ટ	la	લ
tha	ઠ	va	વ
da	ડ	śa	શ
dha	ઢ	ṣa	ષ
na	ણ	sa	સ
ta	ત	ha	હ
tha	થ	la	ળ

Gujarati vowels

a	અ	ri	ઋ
ā	આ	e,ē	એ
i	ઇ	oi,ai	ઐ
ī	ઈ	o,ō	ઓ
u	ઉ	ou,au	ઔ
ū	ઊ		

Alphabets

Oriya consonants

k	କ୍	ṭa	ଟ	ya	ଯ
kh	ଖ୍	ṭha	ଠ	ra	ର
g	ଗ୍	ḍa	ଡ	ḷa	ଳ
gh	ଘ୍	ḍha	ଢ	ba	ବ
ṅ	ଙ୍	ṇa	ଣ	śa	ଶ
ka	କ	ta	ତ	ṣa	ଷ
kha	ଖ	tha	ଥ	sa	ସ
ga	ଗ	da	ଦ	ha	ହ
gha	ଘ	dha	ଧ	ṁ	ଂ
ṅa	ଙ	na	ନ	ḥ	ଃ
cha	ଚ	pa	ପ	ñ	ଁ
chha	ଛ	pha	ଫ	ṛa	ଡ଼
ja	ଜ	ba	ବ	ṛha	ଢ଼
jha	ଝ	bha	ଭ	la	ଳ
ña	ଞ	ma	ମ୍	ya	ଯ

Oriya vowels

a	ଅ	u	ଉ	e,ē	ଏ
ā	ଆ	ū	ଊ	ai,oi	ଐ
i	ଇ	ru	ଋ	o,ō	ଓ
ī	ଈ	rū	ୠ	ou	ଔ

59

Difficult-to-identify stamps

The following pages picture stamps that are particularly difficult to identify. These stamps are organized primarily according to their inscriptions. For example, stamps bearing inscriptions in a language used predominantly in Europe are illustrated under European language inscriptions. This category is further subdivided into Romance languages (French, Italian, Spanish and Portuguese), Germanic languages, Eastern European languages, Cyrillic and Greek.

A stamp may be pictured under "European language inscriptions" even though the issuing country may not be located in Europe. For example, a stamp issued by Libya is shown under "Romance languages, French" because the inscription on the stamp is in French. Another stamp from Libya is pictured under "Romance languages, Italian" because it is inscribed "Poste Italiane."

The collector who has a stamp with an inscription in French is more likely to look for the stamp among French stamps or among stamps with similar inscriptions. He is more likely to look among Italian stamps for a stamp with a "Poste Italiane" inscription. For this reason, the editors of the *Linn's Stamp Identifier* grouped together stamps with similar inscriptions even though the issuing countries may be from different parts of the world.

Similarly, stamps with Arabic inscriptions are pictured together. The same holds true for Asian inscriptions. Because collectors may have difficulty distinguishing between Cyrillic characters and Greek characters, illustrations of stamps bearing Cyrillic and Greek inscriptions are grouped together.

If the stamp doesn't fall into a particular language-inscription category, it is pictured according to its use (bogus issue, local, seal and label, telegraph stamp) or the area to which the issuing country belongs (Africa, North America, South and Central America). Stamps showing no name of the issuing country or any other distinguishing inscription are listed under "No country name."

Africa

Dahomey airmail issue

French Equatorial Africa

**Ivory Coast - Vichy airmail
semipostal. Not listed in Scott.**

Liberia specimen

**South Africa definitive
used as a revenue. Not
listed in Scott.**

**Spanish Morocco
(Tangier)**

Arabic inscriptions

Afghanistan   **Afghanistan**   **Afghanistan Official**

Afghanistan postal tax stamp   **Afghanistan postal tax stamp**

Bateken cinderella   **Israel**

Iran   **Iran**   **Iran parcel post stamp**

Difficult-to-identify stamps
Arabic inscriptions

Latakia

Lebanon postal tax stamp

Libya

Libya

Manama - not listed in Scott.

Morocco - currency. Stamplike size and design on thin cardboard. No postal use. Not listed in Scott.

Morocco - Cherifien Local Post. Not listed in Scott.

Arabic inscriptions

**Oman, State of - bogus issue. Not
listed in Scott.**

Pakistan

Pakistan - Bahawalpur Official

Saudi Arabia

Saudi Arabia

Arabic inscriptions

Saudi Arabia

Saudi Arabia postal tax stamp

Somalia

Spanish Morocco Railway Workers charity seal. Not listed in Scott.

Sudan

Syria - Arabian Government

Arabic inscriptions
Turkish

Turkey

Turkey

Turkey

Turkey

Turkey

Turkey

Turkey

Arabic inscriptions
Turkish

Turkey **Turkey** **Turkey semipostal**

**Turkey military stamp -
Army in Thessaly**

**Turkey - Constan-
tinople - local post.
Not listed in Scott.**

Turkey postage due

Turkish Cyprus revenue

**Turkish Naval League label. Not
listed in Scott. Five values of this
label were overprinted for postage in
1921 for Turkey in Asia. These are
listed as Scott 59-63.**

Asian characters and inscriptions

Burma

Burma

Burma

Burma

China

China

China

China postage due

China military stamp

China

Asian characters and inscriptions

China parcel post

China revenue

Chinese rice revenue

China, People's Republic

China, People's Republic

China, People's Republic - Central China

China - Northeastern Province

China, People's Republic - East China

China, People's Republic - East China

Asian characters and inscriptions

China, Republic of

China, Republic of,
specimen

France - Offices in
China - Tchongking

France - Offices in
China - Kwangchowan

Hong Kong revenue.
Not listed in Scott.

Japan

Japan

Japan

Asian characters and inscriptions

Japan airmail

Japan airmail

**Japan specimen.
Not listed in Scott.**

**Japan revenue. Not
listed in Scott.**

**Japan -
Offices in Korea**

Asian characters and inscriptions

Korea

Korea

Korea

Korea revenue. Not listed in Scott.

Korea, Democratic People's Republic

Malaya

Malaya

Manchukuo

Manchukuo

Asian characters and inscriptions

Manchukuo

Manchukuo

Manchukuo

Philippines

**Private charity seal.
Not listed in Scott.**

Ryukyus

Ryukyus

Ryukyus

Ryukyus

Asian characters and inscriptions

Shanghai postal stationery cutout. Not listed in Scott.

Thailand

Thailand

Thailand

Thailand

Asian characters and inscriptions
Indian characters

Nepal

Nepal

Nepal

Azad Hind - "Free India" - privately prepared but not issued. Not listed in Scott.

Asian characters and inscriptions
Indian States

**Convention States -
Gwalior**

Bhor

Bhor

Charkhari

Faridkot

Faridkot

Asian characters and inscriptions

Indian States

Faridkot

Faridkot revenue. Not listed in Scott.

Hyderabad

Hyderabad

Jhalawar

Jind

Morvi

Nowanuggur

Asian characters and inscriptions

Indian States

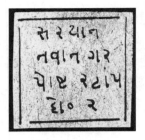

Nowanuggur

Nowanuggur

Nowanuggur

Rajpeepla

Soruth

Travancore

Bogus issues and cinderellas

Czechoslovakia cinderella. Not listed in Scott.

Ireland - Principality of Thomond bogus issue. Not listed in Scott.

Nagaland bogus issue. Not listed in Scott.

South Kasai bogus issue. Not listed in Scott.

South Moluccas bogus issue. Not listed in Scott.

United States fantasy issue. No such flight. Not listed in Scott.

Upper Yaffa bogus issue. Not listed in Scott.

European language inscriptions
Romance languages
French

Andorra, French

Belgium provisional postage due. Not listed in Scott.

Great Britain - Offices in Turkey

France

France - 1942 issue for Anti-Bolshevik Legion fighting with Germans on the Eastern Front. Not listed in Scott.

French Colonies postage due

Ivory Coast - Vichy airmail semipostal. Not listed in Scott.

Ivory Coast - Vichy semipostal. Not listed in Scott.

European language inscriptions

Romance languages
French

**Katanga 1960 defini-
tive overprinted on
Belgian Congo stamp.
Not listed in Scott.**

Libya

Luxembourg

**Poland - issued under
German occupation**

**Reunion - Vichy issue.
Not listed in Scott.**

Reunion postage due

**Reproduction of Suez
Canal Company local.
Not listed in Scott.**

**Tunisia - officially
perfined for
postage due**

81

European language inscriptions

Romance languages
Italian

Italy pneumatic post

Italy - postal statio-
nery cutout. Same
design as contempo-
rary definitive. Not
listed in Scott.

Italy - 1943 Republi-
can National Guard
overprint. Not listed in
Scott.

Libya

Vatican City - postal
stationery cutout. Not
listed in Scott.

San Marino parcel post stamps

European language inscriptions

Romance languages
Spanish and Portuguese

Angra

Mexico - Porte de Mar
stamp

Peru

Peru

Philippines newspaper
stamp surcharged as a
revenue stamp. Not
listed in Scott.

Portugal

Portuguese Africa

83

European language inscriptions

Romance languages
Spanish and Portuguese

Spain

Spain

Spain

Spain

Spain - Zaragoza charity seal. Not
listed in Scott.

Spain - 1934 postal charity seal.
Not listed in Scott.

Spain - 1937 postal
charity seal. Not listed
in Scott.

European language inscriptions

Romance languages
Spanish and Portuguese

Spain - 1944 postal charity seal.
Not listed in Scott.

Spain - Civil War -
1936 local post stamp
for Durcal (Grenada).
Not listed in Scott.

Spain - 1963 postal
tax stamp for
Valencia. Not listed in
Scott.

Spain war tax stamp

Uruguay

Uruguay

Venezuela

European language inscriptions

Germanic languages

Austria

Austria

Austria postage due

Austria newspaper
stamp overprinted "T"
for use as postage due.
Not listed in Scott.

Austria military stamp

Austria military
newspaper stamp

Belgium - issued under
German occupation

Bosnia & Herzegovina
semipostal

European language inscriptions

Germanic languages

Danube Steam & Navigation
Company. Not listed in
Scott.

Danzig

France - issued under
German occupation

German States - Thurn &
Taxis (Northern District)

German States -
Bavaria

Germany - North
German Confederation

Germany semipostal

87

European language inscriptions

Germanic languages

Germany Official   **Germany Official**   **Germany - local Official stamp (for use in Prussia)**

Germany - 1948 postal tax stamp for Berlin relief. Not listed in Scott.   **Germany bill of lading revenue. Not listed in Scott.**

Germany bill of exchange revenue. Not listed in Scott.   **Germany, Berlin - specimen**

European language inscriptions

Germanic languages

Netherlands postal stationery cutout. Not listed in Scott.

Netherlands - postage due stamp

Norway

Norway

Poland - issued under German occupation

Romania - issued under Austrian occupation

Romania - issued under German occupation

Russia - Wenden

European language inscriptions

Germanic languages

Saar

Saar

Siberia Official

Sweden postage due

Switzerland - 1912
semiofficial charity
stamp for youth
charities

European language inscriptions

Eastern European languages

Albania

Albania

Albania

**Albania, government in exile -
bogus issue. Not listed in Scott.**

Bohemia & Moravia semipostal

European language inscriptions

Eastern European languages

**Central Lithuania
postage due**

Croatia

Croatia

Croatia

Croatia semipostal

Estonia

European language inscriptions

Eastern European languages

**Estonia - occupation
semipostal**

Georgia

Hungary

Hungary semipostal

**Hungary - issued
under French
occupation**

**Hungary - issued under
Romanian occupation**

**Hungary - issued under
Romanian occupation**

European language inscriptions

Eastern European languages

Latvia

Lithuania
(Baltic States)

Lithuania

Lithuania imperf pair (mock perfs)

Lithuania

Moldova

Moldova

European language inscriptions
Eastern European languages

North Ingermanland

Poland Official

Romania

Romania postal tax stamp issued under German occupation

Romania - Offices in the Turkish Empire

Romania - revenue overprinted for use under German World War I occupation. Not listed in Scott.

Slovakia

Slovenia

European language inscriptions

Eastern European languages

Yugoslavia postage due stamp for
Bosnia and Herzegovina

Yugoslavia - Croatia-
Slavonia

Yugoslavia - Ljubljana -
German occupation

Yugoslavia - Ljubljana -
German occupation

Europe

Cyrillic and Greek

**Albania -
bogus Mirdities issue. Not
listed in Scott.**

Armenia

Armenia

Armenia

Armenia

Armenia

Armenia

Europe

Cyrillic and Greek

Armenia

Armenia

Azerbaijan

**Azerbaijan - bogus.
Not listed in Scott.**

Batum

Belarus

Bulgaria

Europe

Cyrillic and Greek

Bulgaria   **Bulgaria**   **Bulgaria**

Bulgaria

Bulgaria

Bulgaria

Europe

Cyrillic and Greek

**Central Lithuania
postage due**

**Czechoslovakia - printed for
use in Carpatho-Ukraine but
issued in Prague at the
same time**

**Czechoslovak Legion
Post**

Far Eastern Republic

Far Eastern Republic

Far Eastern Republic

Far Eastern Republic

Far Eastern Republic

Europe

Cyrillic and Greek

Finland

Finland military stamp

Georgia

Georgia semipostal

Georgia - "Day of the National Guard, 12-12-1920" overprint on remainder of Scott 15. Overprinted in Italy after Red occupation. Not listed in Scott.

Kazakhstan

Kyrgyzstan

Europe
Cyrillic and Greek

Latvia - 1919 Western Army (unissued with later overprint). Not listed in Scott.

Montenegro

Montenegro

Montenegro

Montengro postage due

Montenegro postage due

Odessa Famine Relief - privately produced for collectors. Not listed in Scott.

102

Europe

Cyrillic and Greek

Poland

Russia

Russia

Russia

Russia

Russia

Russia

Russia

Russia

Russia

Russia

Russia

Russia

Russia

Russia semipostal

Russia semipostal

Europe

Cyrillic and Greek

**Russia - Offices
in China**

**Russia - Offices
in China**

**Russia - Offices in the
Turkish Empire**

**Russia - Offices in the
Turkish Empire**

**Russia - Offices in the
Turkish Empire**

Russia - Wrangel issue

**Russia revenue
authorized for postal
use in 1909. Not listed
in Scott.**

**Russia revenue. Not
listed in Scott.**

Serbia

Europe

Cyrillic and Greek

Serbia

Serbia

Serbia

Serbia postage due

Serbia Official - issued
under German
occupation

Siberia

Siberia

Siberia

Siberia

Europe

Cyrillic and Greek

Slovakia

South Russia

South Russia

South Russia

Tajikistan

Tajikistan

Tannu Tuva

Tannu Tuva

Europe

Cyrillic and Greek

Transcaucasia

Transcaucasia

Transcaucasia

Turkestan - circa 1921 - bogus. Not listed in Scott.

Turkestan - circa 1921 - bogus. Not listed in Scott.

Turkestan - circa 1921 - bogus. Not listed in Scott.

Europe

Cyrillic and Greek

Turkmenistan

Ukraine

Ukraine

Ukraine

Ukraine

Ukraine

Ukraine

Ukraine - provisional paper currency. Not a stamp. Not listed in Scott. A provisional stamp features the same design but is imperforate.

109

Europe

Cyrillic and Greek

Ukraine

Ukraine

Ukraine

Ukraine

Ukraine

Ukraine semipostal

**Ukraine - unissued.
Not listed in Scott.**

**Ukraine - overprint
applied by favor. Not
listed in Scott.**

Europe

Cyrillic and Greek

Uzbekistan

Uzbekistan

Western Army of General Aralov-Bermondt. Not issued. Not listed in Scott. Forgeries exist.

Western Ukraine

Western Ukraine - bogus overprint on Ukrainian stamp. Not listed in Scott.

White Russia - not issued. Likely a propaganda label. Not listed in Scott.

Europe

Cyrillic and Greek

Yugoslavia

Yugoslavia

Yugoslavia semipostal

Yugoslavia
postal tax stamp

Yugoslavia postal
stationery cutout. Not
listed in Scott.

Yugoslavia - Bosnia
and Herzegovia

Yugoslavia - Bosnia and
Herzegovia

Europe
Cyrillic and Greek

Yugoslavia semipostal
for Carinthia
Plebiscite

Yugoslavia - Croatia-
Slavonia

Yugoslavia - Slovenia

Yugoslavia - Slovenia

Yugoslavia - Slovenia

Yugoslavia - Ljubljana
- Italian occupation

Yugoslavia - Istria and the
Slovene Coast (Zone B)

Yugoslavia - Trieste
(Zone B)

113

Europe
Cyrillic and Greek

**Crete - Russian sphere
of administration -
District of Rethymnon**

Epirus

Greece

Greece

**Greece
postal tax stamp**

Thrace

**Thrace - issued under
Greek occupation**

Locals

Lundy Island local. Not listed in Scott.

Lundy Island local.
Not listed in Scott.

Norway - Arendals
Bypost. Not listed in
Scott.

Norway - Arendals
Bypost. Not listed in
Scott.

Norway - Trodheim
local. Not listed in
Scott.

No country name

Austria

Austria newspaper stamp

Austria newspaper stamp

**Austria - Offices in the
Turkish Empire**

**Bosnia and
Herzegovina**

**Bosnia and
Herzegovina**

**Bosnia and
Herzegovina
newspaper stamp**

No country name

Germany - Russian occupation - East Saxony

Great Britain

Great Britain

Great Britain postal stationery cutout. Not listed in Scott.

Great Britain Contract Note fiscal. Not listed in Scott.

Great Britain Inland Revenue fiscal. Not listed in Scott.

Italy postal card cutout. Not listed in Scott.

Montenegro - Government in Exile acknowledgment of receipt stamp, circa 1920. Not listed in Scott.

117

No country name

Peru forgery. Not
listed in Scott.

Netherlands   **Norway Official**

Peru   **Peru postage due**

Peru postal tax stamp   **Portugal postage due**

No country name

Spain Official

Switzerland postage due

Switzerland - postal stationery cutout. Not listed in Scott.

Venezuela

Yugoslavia - Bosnia and Herzegovia

North America

Canada - postal stationery
cutout. Same design as
contemporary definitive
series except enlarged. Not
listed in Scott.

Canada bill revenue.
Not listed in Scott.

United States

United States War
Savings stamp

United States Insur-
ance stamp - probably
for use in premium
booklet. Not listed
in Scott.

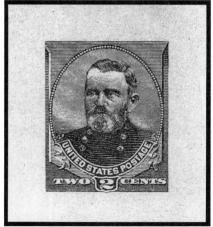

United States lettersheet

United States Consular
Service fee revenue

Seals and labels

**Australia airmail etiquette.
Not listed in Scott.**

**Colombia tuberculosis seal.
Not listed in Scott.**

**Denmark
Christmas seal.
Not listed in Scott.**

**Italy airmail etiquette. Not listed
in Scott.**

**Israel fund-raising labels for
Jewish school in Jerusalem.
Not listed in Scott.**

121

Seals and labels

United States post office seal

**United States - Independent Postal Service of America.
Not listed in Scott.**

South and Central America

**Argentina specimen.
Not listed in Scott.**

**Bolivia - unissued 1894 stamp,
part of a nine-value set. Not listed
in Scott.**

**Bolivia - crude imitation of 1894
unissued set. Not listed in Scott.**

Chile

**Chile Telegraph stamp. Not
listed in Scott.**

123

South and Central America

Colombia
publicity label. Not
listed in Scott.

Cuba

Ecuador postal tax
stamp

Ecuador Telegraph stamp.
Not listed in Scott.

Ecuador Telegraph stamp.
Not listed in Scott.

Ecuador fiscal over-
print for postal use.
Not listed in Scott.

Mexico
Tuberculosis seal. Not
listed in Scott.

Nicaragua - postal
stationery cutout -
same design as
contemporary defini-
tive series. Not listed
in Scott.

Telegraph stamps

Switzerland. Not listed in Scott.

United States

United States

United States

United States

United States

United States

United States

United States

125

Overprints and surcharges

These overprints and surcharges indicate a different country from the issuing country of the basic unoverprinted or unsurcharged stamp.

Overprints on Bosnia & Herzegovina stamps

КРАЉЕВСТВО

C. X. C.

КРАЉЕВСТВО
СРБА, ХРВАТА
И СЛОВЕНАЦА

40

40 хелера 40

ПОРТО

5 X

ДРЖАВА С.Х.С.
БОСНА И
ХЕРЦЕГОВИНА

Yugoslavia

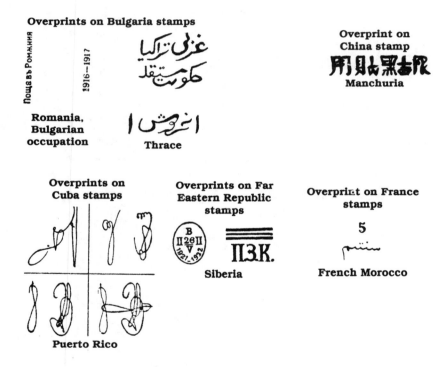

Overprints on Bulgaria stamps

ПОЩВ ВЪ РОМЖНИЯ

1916—1917

**Romania,
Bulgarian
occupation**

Thrace

**Overprint on
China stamp**

Manchuria

**Overprints on
Cuba stamps**

Puerto Rico

**Overprints on Far
Eastern Republic
stamps**

ПЗК.

Siberia

**Overprint on France
stamps**

5

French Morocco

Overprints on French Colonies stamps

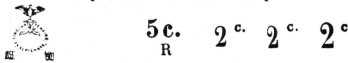

5 c.
R

2 c. 2 c. 2 c.

New Caledonia

Reunion

Overprints on Germany stamps

Österreich

Austria

Freistaat Bayern

German
States,
Bavaria

Elsaß Lothringen

3 Cent. **1 S**

✱ **1F.25Cent.** ✱

France, German
occupation

**Russisch-
Polen**

Gen.-Gouv
Warschau

Poland, German
occupation

M.V.i.R
25 Bani

Rumänien
25 Bani

Romania, German
occupation

Overprints on Great Britain stamps

Rialtar
Sealabac
na
héireann
1922

Saorstát
éireann
1922

Ireland

Overprints on Greece stamps

**ΔΙΟΙΚΗΣΙΣ
ΔΥΤΙΚΗΣ
ΘΡΑΚΗΣ**

Διοίκησις
Θραχης

Thrace

Overprint on India stamps

Oman (Muscat)

Overprints on Japan stamps

叁 暫
圓 定
郵替機華香

臺圓 暫
鳧鎮 定
郵替機華方

オネルボ北

North Borneo,
Japanese occupation

조 선
우표
5 전

Korea,
U.S. military rule

Hong Kong, Japanese
occupation

Handstamped on Japan stamps

**Ryukyu Islands,
U.S. administration**

Overprint on Japan (Formosa) stamps

臺 中
灣 華
省 民
 國

China, Taiwan

Overprint on Lourenco Marques stamps

10 C.

with or without:

PORTEADO

Mozambique

Overprints on Palestine stamps

Jordan (Transjordan)

Overprints on Russia stamps

Armenia

200 000 эдб.

Georgia

2p.50к.

Р. 5 Р.

Д. В.
коп. 1 коп.

золотом

Far Eastern Republic

South Russia

35

Siberia

1
рубль

Siberia

+

Far Eastern Republic

+

Siberia

Armenia with added overprint:

Transcaucasian Federated Republics

Ukraine

128

**Overprints on Russia,
South Russia or Ukraine
stamps**

ПОЧТА
РУССКОЙ
АРМІИ
—
1.000
РУБЛЕЙ

РУССКАЯ
ПОЧТА
10,000
РУБЛЕЙ.

**Russia, Offices in
Turkey**

**Overprints on
stamps of
Russia, Offices
in Turkey**

Р. О. П. и Т.

**Ukraine, private
overprint.
Overprinted
stamps were not
issued.**

Overprints on Saudi Arabia (Hejaz) stamps

**Overprint on Serbia
stamps**

Демократска
Федеративна
Jугославиja

+3

**Overprint on Serbia,
German occupation
stamps**

Демократска
Федеративна
Jугославиja
Yugoslavia

Jordan (Transjordan)

129

Overprints on Turkey stamps

Greece

ΓΚΙΟΥΜΟΥ
ΛΤΖΙΝΑΣ
ΛΕΠΤΑ 25

Thrace

Υπάτη Αρμοστεία
Θρακης
5 Λεπτὰ 5

**Thrace, Greek
occupation**

Saudi Arabia (Nejd)

Syria, Arabian Government

Many Arabic overprints on stamps of Turkey are issues from Turkey-in-Asia or early Egypt.

**Surcharge on
Yugoslavia stamps**

Serbia

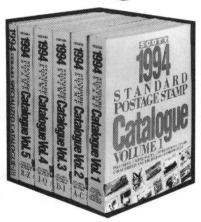

Key to map on cover

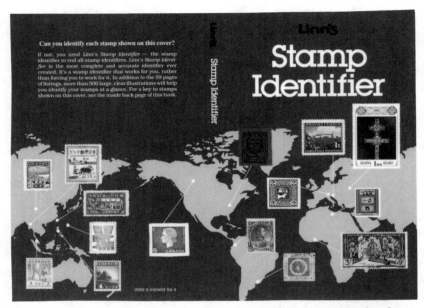

The stamps shown on the cover were issued by the following countries: front cover, clockwise, beginning with stamp showing cross, Belarus; yellow stamp with "5," Libya; red 3f+9f stamp, Ivory Coast Vichy semipostal (not listed in Scott); Montevideo 60 centesimos, Uruguay; green 5 centimos, Venezuela; blue stamp with head and "2," Austria; Pacific Mutual stamp, United States; Provinz Laibach stamp, Yugoslavia Ljubljana; back cover, clockwise, beginning with red stamp showing soldiers, China; stamp showing farmer plowing, Burma; "3.00" stamp, Republic of China; 2¢ stamp, Ryukyus; 5¢ stamp portraying Queen Elizabeth II, Canada postal stationery cutout (not listed in Scott); "4" green stamp, Philippines; 3¢ stamp, Malaya.